An Altitude SuperGuide

Kananaskis

by Ward Cameron

●

Altitude Publishing Canada Ltd.
Canadian Rockies/Vancouver

Publication Information

Altitude Publishing Canada Ltd.

1500 Railway Avenue, PO Box 1410
Canmore, Alberta T0L 0M0

Canadian Cataloguing in Publication Data

Cameron, Ward, 1961-
    Kananaskis

    (SuperGuide)
    Includes index.
    ISBN 1-55153-610-2

1. Kananaskis Country (Alta.)--Guidebooks.
2. Natural history--Alberta--Kananaskis Country--Guidebooks. 3. Outdoor recreation--Alberta--Kananaskis Country--Guidebooks. I. Title.
II. Series.
FC3695.K36C35 1996 917.123'32043 C96-910289-5
F1079.K36C35 1996

9 8 7 6 5 4 3 2 1

Made in Western Canada

Printed and bound in Canada
by Friesen Printers, Altona, Manitoba.

Altitude GreenTree Program

Altitude Publishing will plant in Canada twice as many trees as were used in the manufacturing of this product.

Front cover photo: Mount Kidd

Inset front cover: Bald eagle

Frontispiece: Ribbon Creek Trail

Back cover photo: Upper Kananaskis Lake and Mount Sarrail

Project Development

Concept/Art Direction	Stephen Hutchings
Design	Stephen Hutchings
Editing	Penny E. Grey
Index/Proofreading	Noeline Bridge
Maps	Catherine Burgess
Drawings	Stephen Hutchings
Text Processing	Tracy Whillans
FPO Scanning	Tracy Whillans
Electronic Page Layout	Sandra Davis
Financial Management	Laurie Smith

A Note from the Publisher

The world described in Altitude SuperGuides is a unique and fascinating place. It is a world filled with surprise and discovery, beauty and enjoyment, questions and answers. It is a world of people, cities, landscape, animals, and wilderness as seen through the eyes of those who live in, work with, and care for this world. The process of describing this world is also a means of defining ourselves.

It is also a world of relationship, where people derive their meaning from a deep and abiding contact with the land–as well as from each other. And it is this sense of relationship that guides all of us at Altitude to ensure that these places continue to survive and evolve in the decades ahead.

Altitude SuperGuides are books intended to be used, as much as read. Like the world they describe, Altitude SuperGuides are evolving, adapting and growing. Please write to us with your comments and observations, and we will do our best to incorporate your ideas into future editions of these books.

Stephen Hutchings

Stephen Hutchings
Publisher

An Altitude SuperGuide

Kananaskis

Contents

The **Kananaskis SuperGuide** is organized according to the following colour scheme:

Information and introductory sections. . . . .

The Kananaskis Trail (Hwy. 40). . . . .

Peter Lougheed Provincial Park . . . .

The Smith–Dorrien/Spray Trail . . . .

Bow Valley Provincial Park. . . . .

Sibbald Creek Trail. . . . .

The Elbow Falls Trail (Hwy. 66) . . . .

Sheep Valley. . . . .

1. Introduction

Mount Baldy towers above Highway 40

Welcome to Alberta's best-kept secret. Kananaskis Country, a 4,000-sq.-km (1,600-sq.-mi.) recreation area, contains the highest driveable point in Canada, the highest hiking trail in the Canadian Rockies, world-class golf courses, five-star hotels, horseback, mountain-bike and four-wheel-drive trails, and even a former prisoner-of-war camp.

A virtual newborn when compared to the 100-year history of Banff National Park, Kananaskis Country has nevertheless become an area of unparalleled alpine recreation. In 1977, then premier Peter Lougheed set aside 4,000 sq. km (1,600 sq. mi.) of Alberta's eastern Rocky Mountain slopes as Kananaskis Country Provincial Recreation Area. In addition, an area of 304 sq. km (122 sq. mi.) around the Kananaskis Lakes was preserved within the newly estab-

lished Kananaskis Provincial Park (now Peter Lougheed Provincial Park). Geographically, Kananaskis Country is west of Calgary, Alberta and borders Banff National Park and the Continental Divide on its western margin.

Not a park, Kananaskis Country is managed using a multiple-use concept, allowing it to support a wide variety of activities. Planners unleashed on this new area divided it based on sensitivity to impact. Delicate areas were classed as "prime protection," whereas others were zoned to allow development. Also, four provin-

cial parks lie within this large area: Peter Lougheed, Bow Valley, and Bragg Creek provincial parks, along with the newly established Elbow–Sheep Wildland Park.

Kananaskis Country straddles the transition from foothill to mountain. This provides a dramatic landscape, and a varied plant and animal population. From the white-tail deer of the plains to the alpine-dwelling mountain goat, a considerable variety of wildlife can be viewed from within its boundaries.

Over the years, the Kananaskis has seen many vis-

Opposite: Wedge Pond and The Wedge

itors. In its early days, it was used as a travel corridor for the early settlers of the Oregon Territory. Later, during the Great Depression, a camp provided work for the multitudes of the unemployed. Like many in such camps across North America, these workers built some of the earliest recreational developments in the area. As the Depression ended and war approached, the camp was taken over for internment of German nationals. It was later converted into a full-fledged prisoner-of-war camp.

Once the prisoners were repatriated, the valley returned to a quiet existence, until its formal designation in 1977. Even then, things remained relatively peaceful, as marketing outside the province was almost non-existent. This all changed in 1988 with the Calgary Winter Olympics. Since both the downhill and Nordic events were held within the boundaries of Kananaskis Country, millions of people were introduced to this area. Subsequently, the Kananaskis has been the focus of media attention and endless numbers of development proposals. At the same time, it provides some of the most spectacular scenery and extensive outdoor recreation in the Rockies.

How To Use This Book

Kananaskis Country, with its well-developed roads and facilities, offers picturesque panoramas, quiet campgrounds, and scenic Sunday drives. It has something for every type of outdoor enthusiast, whether technical rock climbing or more passive pursuits. This book is designed to provide a general introduction to the area—its recreational potential and scenic highlights. At the same time, it is designed to facilitate browsing and allow serendipity to take over.

To maintain some semblance of order, it has been divided into sections. After this introductory chapter, chapter two provides a general description of the natural history of the Kananaskis. The mountains are unique, with features and processes that aren't found elsewhere. Plants and animals must be capable of surviving a harsh environment.

Chapter three looks at the human history of this amazing area. Though the plants and animals have had hundreds of generations to adapt to the harsh realities of mountain life, the area's non-indigenous residents have had only a few. The short time of non-native involvement provides a surprising number of anecdotes of struggle and exploration.

The mountains beg to be explored, and personally experienced. Kananaskis is a unique playground with opportunities for just about any wilderness activity; there are places for quiet hikes, or screaming dirt bikes. The camping facilities are endless, and the backcountry beckons. Chapter four describes some of the opportunities for recreation. It is merely a primer on some of the options available, and will help you make more of your trip to the Kananaskis.

The remainder of the book has been divided based on region. Most visitors to Kananaskis Country explore one region at a time due its expansive nature and widely spaced access points. Since the Kananaskis Trail (Highway 40) is the most visited and extensively explored corridor, the book starts there. From the Kananaskis Trail, it moves to other areas in the following order: Peter Lougheed Provincial Park, the Smith–Dorrien/Spray Trail, Bow Valley Provincial Park, Sibbald Creek Trail, the Elbow Falls Trail, and finally the Sheep River Valley.

One challenge of writing a book on the Kananaskis comes from the planner's habit of naming roads "Trails." Roads like the Powderface Trail are often confused by true trail names like Powderface Ridge Trail, or Powderface Creek Trail. When necessary, the word "road" will be added to the names of highways to avoid confusion.

As you explore Kananaskis Country, you will undoubtedly find that the area's diversity and rugged nature, in addition to its spectacular beauty, will draw you back again and again.

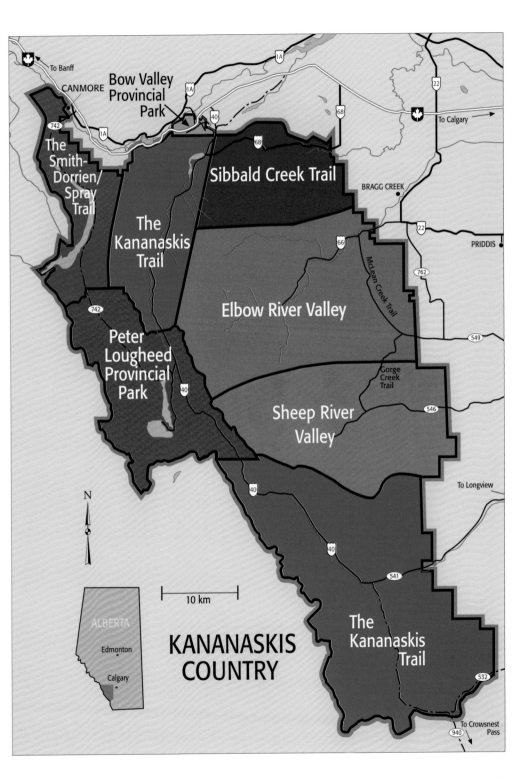

To Banff

CANMORE

Bow Valley
Provincial
Park

To Calgary

The
Smith-
Dorrien/
Spray
Trail

Sibbald Creek Trail

BRAGG CREEK

The
Kananaskis
Trail

PRIDDIS

McLean Creek Trail

Elbow River Valley

Peter
Lougheed
Provincial
Park

Gorge
Creek
Trail

Sheep River
Valley

To Longview

N

10 km

ALBERTA

Edmonton

Calgary

KANANASKIS
COUNTRY

The
Kananaskis
Trail

To Crowsnest
Pass

2. Highlights of Nature

Sunset over the Elk Range

Kananaskis Country's landscape is a unique combination of prairie, foothill, and mountain. Plains give way to the jagged peaks of the Rocky Mountains, and the plants and animals reflect this diversity. The eastern part of Kananaskis Country exhibits the rolling character of the foothills, with a gentle transition from valley to ridgetop. Primarily sandstone and shale, these low, tree-covered slopes support a diverse plant and animal life. They also form an ideal terrain for recreational pursuits like mountain biking and horseback riding. The valleys are normally composed of soft shale surrounded by resistant ridges of sandstone. The youngest of the Kananaskis rock structures, they range in age from 135–75 million years.

The western ends of the Elbow and Sheep river valleys mark the official start of the Front Ranges of the Rocky Mountains. Particularly evident along Highway 66, the rolling face of Powderface Ridge stands in stark contrast to the jagged knife-blade appearance of Nihahi Ridge. Climbing Nihahi Ridge, you see only jagged peaks to the west and rolling foothills to the east.

The Front Ranges are characterized by steeply angled slopes with extensive folding. Good places to see these slopes are along the Opal, Highwood, and Kananaskis ranges.

Further west, the jagged peaks of the Front Ranges give way to the higher, more castellate summits of the Main Ranges. These resistant slopes are made of ancient limestones and dolomites, the oldest rocks in the Kananaskis area.

Kananaskis' combination of plains mixed with foothills and mountains makes it an ideal place to study natural history. By following the transition of aspen parkland to rocky alpine ridges, you find a larger variety of plants and animals than by travelling either east to the plains or deeper into the mountains.

The mountain climate also has an effect on the plants and animals. When the steep,

Opposite: Subalpine larch adds autumn colours to the slopes of Mount Birdwood

Life Before the Mountains

Mounts Sarrail, Foch, and Fox above the Upper Kananaskis Lake

THE MOUNTAINS DIDN'T always exist as they do today; 345 million years ago, much of western Canada was submerged beneath the waves of a large inland sea. Within these waters, thick beds of limestone were deposited. Today this limestone is a major component of the Rocky Mountains. We can see stark limestone formations in the cliffs above the Kananaskis Lakes and Mount Birdwood along the Smith–Dorrien/Spray Trail.

By 156 million years ago, the seas had receded and been replaced by a swampy lowland. To the southwest was a large sea, whose shoreline changed over time. In the shallow waters, limestone, siltstone, and sandstone formed. In the deeper waters farther from shore, fine clays settled to the bottom, forming extensive layers of shale.

In time, the oceans receded, and by 65 million years ago, warm temperate conditions prevailed, with large rivers meandering across the plains, bringing sediments from low mountains to the west. Daily, across Alberta, the age-old struggle for survival

continued as it had for eons. Huge meat-eating dinosaurs, like *Albertasaurus,* were patrolling the edges of marshes and rivers, looking for potential prey. Many left their remains behind, to be dug up as fossils in Alberta's dinosaur country. Most of the fine-grained sandstone, siltstone, and shale, created over wide areas of land, were later removed by erosion, and none remain within Kananaskis.

To understand the formation of the Rockies, we need to examine a theory known as Plate Tectonics. According to this theory, the surface of the Earth is made up of a series of plates, each moving relative to the others. At one time, all the continents were joined into one large land mass. Slowly this supercontinent began to break apart into numerous plates, and the continents began to drift.

Periods of mountain building are known as Orogenys, and in this area two have been responsible for the mountains we see today. Prior to these, the North American Plate had been moving in a westerly direction, and the

neighbouring Pacific Plate trending northward.

As the two plates collided, shock waves moved inland, compressing and piling up the rocks to the east of the impact. The first shock wave initiated the Columbia Orogeny (forming the Columbia Mountains, made up of the Caribous, Selkirks, Purcells, and Monashees), and occurred about 175 million years ago. As the shock wave moved eastward, it forced huge masses of rock to crack and slide up over their neighbours. This thrust faulting was instrumental in the formation of the Rockies. The shock wave began pushing up the western ranges, and then the Main Ranges, about 120 million years ago.

The second shock wave moved inland about 85 million years ago, and touched off the Laramide Orogeny. The force behind this second collision formed the Front Ranges and the foothills, but died out as it approached present-day Calgary, and so the prairies were left undisturbed.

rocky mountains are mixed with a dry, continental climate, we find an environment where only the strong survive. Under difficult conditions, plants and animals become uniquely adapted, and luck is often a key to survival.

Weathering and Erosion

One of the amazing things about mountains is that they are always changing. No sooner had their heads emerged above the waves, when nature began to slowly tear them down. Erosion has taken the original peaks of the Rockies and created a "work in progress," a landscape of ever changing, slowly shrinking peaks.

When the Front Ranges were formed about 75–85 million years ago, they were quite a bit larger than they are today—almost twice the size. A variety of forces are at work.

Water is the biggest agent of erosion, flowing down the

Glacier Cooled

Glaciers changed the landscape

GLACIERS ARE THE most recognizable force helping to shape the mountains. During the ice age, the entire landscape of Alberta changed. Across the prairies huge sheets of ice made their way towards the mountain front, while upslope, rivers of ice were sculpting and scouring the landscape.

Glaciers are a special type of ice. Unlike the brittle ice we are familiar with, glacial ice acts more like a very thick liquid. As glacial ice accumulates into huge masses, pressure on the lower layers allows the ice to flow, slowly, under the force of gravity. The ice on the surface of the glacier isn't under pressure and so remains brittle, and huge crevasses, or cracks, form as it moves over obstacles.

Contrary to popular belief, glaciers are always moving—even during the hottest days of summer—however, they may melt back from the "toe" faster than they move forward. If a glacier moves forward 18 m in a year, but melts backward 23 m during the summer, then the net movement is 5 m up the valley. We call this a receding glacier, and this is the situation for most glaciers in Alberta today.

Glaciers themselves do very little eroding. It's the material carried within the ice that acts as an abrasive, carving away at the valley. Glaciers pick up rocks and debris along their margins, and this material is carried down the valley, forming a powerful abrasive. As you might imagine, these rocks are quickly ground into a fine powder, known as rock flour, which then makes its way into our streams and lakes, giving them the incredible colours known the world over.

Mountain Types

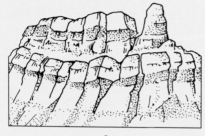

Castellate Mountain
Typically found in the Main Ranges, this type of mountain shows towers composed of horizontal layers of resistant limestone, dolomite, and quartzite, and ledges of softer shale. Mount Kidd is a classic example.

Horn Mountain
Carved by glaciers on several sides, horn mountains are remnant peaks left behind when the glaciers melted.

Sawtooth Mountain
Common in the Front Ranges, sawtooth mountains are formed when steeply angled slopes are carved by the action of wind and water to create jagged ridges similar to the blade of a saw.

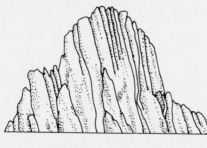

Dogtooth Mountain
Another Front Range mountain, the dogtooth occurs when the layers of a peak are thrust almost straight up leaving a resistant spire appearance. Mount Birdwood is a classic example of such a peak.

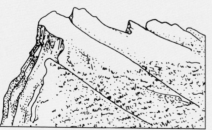

Overthrust Mountain
Often described as a "writing desk" type of mountain, overthrust mountains are a classic Front Range peak. Formerly horizontal layers of rock are thrust up, at steep angles, over younger rocks. Mount Rundle is a classic example, as is Nihahi Ridge in the Elbow Valley of Kananaskis Country.

Big Elbow River and Forget-Me-Not Mountain

mountain as runoff. As it flows, it picks up material, and these sediments in turn act as abrasives that wear away at the rock. Water has a dramatic impact on the landforms we see. Each mountain is being slowly dissected by flowing water. As rivulets give way to rivers, mountain ranges are cut into peaks.

Further downstream, the river may carve intricate canyons and create roaring waterfalls, depending on geological conditions. Water is the chisel with which the mountains are being sculpted.

Constant freezing and thawing works to chip away the mountains. Water expands as it freezes, and when it flows into small cracks and subsequently freezes, it acts as a powerful wedge. When you look at the large, loose-rock, or scree, slopes found at the base of most cliffs in the area, you're looking at the results of millions of years of freezing and thawing.

Much of the scree that makes up these slopes was formed near the end of the last ice age, as areas adjacent to the receding glaciers experienced climatic conditions similar to permafrost areas. This periglacial, or "near glacial" climate resulted in significantly more frost-wedging than today. So for a short time, geologically speaking, the mountains were being worn down at a more rapid rate than they are now.

Chemical erosion is another process acting on the mountains. Water and carbon dioxide in the atmosphere react to form a weak carbonic acid, which easily dissolves the limestone and washes it away.

Plants also help to wear the mountains down. Some, like the orange lichens coating many of the local rocks, can slowly dissolve the rock and help in the creation of soil. Other plants force their roots down the smallest of cracks and cause results similar to those of frost wedging.

By understanding the processes that have helped to shape the mountains, we can more easily interpret the landforms themselves. Each process has distinctive impacts, and helps us to see the process of change, even though we may not notice the mountains visibly shrinking.

Climate

Living in the mountains has its ups and downs—literally. It has the advantage of some of the most dramatic scenery in the world; however, it also requires dealing with weather patterns that vary as dramatically.

The variation in temperature is difficult for most newcomers to comprehend. Sun and shade can vary by as much as 50°F, while daily fluctuations can be even larger. One July day, the high at the Kananaskis Ranger Station was 32.8°C (91.8°F), while the average for July is a more moderate 22.7°C (72.9°F). Temperatures can easily drop below freezing when sudden

Sheep River Valley

storms come through. It is normal for it to snow at high elevations at least once in July each year. In January, the temperature can vary between a frigid -45°C (-49°F) and a balmy 10 (50°F) or 15°C (59°F).

The prevailing winds are generally from the west, and greatly influence the weather. Heading inland from the Pacific coast, they begin as moisture-laden clouds that cool rapidly as they are forced to climb over the mountains. This drop in temperature forces them to release much of their moisture as snow and rain, long before they reach the eastern side of the Divide. Kananaskis would be much wetter were it not for our mountain wall. For instance, Revelstoke has an annual precipitation of around 1,064 mm (43 in.) compared to the 400–600-mm (16–24-in.) average in Kananaskis.

Not to be outdone, the prairies also influence our weather. Despite our normally western winds, we often feel the sting of easterlies during early summer or in the midst of cold winters. Since these clouds are still moisture laden upon reaching the mountains, and cool as they head west, we find ourselves digging out the rain gear. This "upslope weather" can last several weeks at a time, and is characterized by the presence of clear weather on the western side of the Divide. Head west and you may be able to escape the grasp of an upslope storm.

During winter upslope conditions, the weather is usually very dry, and is influenced by the large arctic fronts so well known in the north. We are often left with little precipitation and very cold temperatures. You may also notice ice crystals in the air for extended periods during a cold upslope pattern.

These same slope weather patterns can also occur more locally. Called orographic lifting, water droplets that evaporate during the day, rise and rapidly cool. As the water condenses with increased altitude, you may notice clouds around high summits on otherwise cloudless days.

Along with orographic lifting comes orographic weather. As the air warms during the heat of day, it rises and slowly condenses around the mountain tops. By mid to late afternoon, enough moisture has condensed to cause a sudden, torrential downpour. These storms are usually short lived, and very localized in nature, but can be extremely violent and prone to lightning. It's important to be on the look-out for this type of weather when hiking on hot summer evenings. There have been numerous fatalities caused by lightning. Make sure you drop down off exposed ridges when bad weather comes in. Since the patterns vary with the local geography, moving from one side of a valley to another can mean a huge change in weather.

Chinooks—the "perfect hurricane"

OF THE MANY weather patterns characterizing the Rockies, none are more steeped in mystery and folklore than the Chinook wind. These hot, dry winds are famous for bringing a welcome respite to winter, and for leaving Calgary free of snow in January. The temperature changes can be dramatic. On Jan. 11, 1983, the temperature in Calgary rose 30°C (54°F) (from -17°C to 13°C) in four hours, and on February 7, 1964, the humidity dropped by 43 percent, while the temperature rose 28°C (50.4°F).

To the local Indians, it was known as the "Snow Eater," for it could literally eat a foot of snow per hour. With rapid rises in temperature, snow has little time to melt, so instead, quickly evaporates. To local natives living on the plains during frigid winters, the Chinook was seen as a welcome break from the cold.

The journals of early explorers are filled with details on the Chinook. Alexander MacKenzie referred to a Chinook as a "perfect hurricane." In 1787, David Thompson wrote that the rise in temperature experienced by travelling to the mountains was similar to travelling south. Even at the turn of the century, the *Calgary Herald* was writing about these warm winds.

"Those who have not the warm, invigorating Chinook winds of this country, cannot well comprehend what a blessing they are. The icy

The famous Chinook arch

clutch of winter is lessened, the earth throws off its winding sheet of snow. Humanity ventures forth to inhale the balmy spring like air. Animated nature rejoices." (1900—Calgary weekly Herald)

How does a Chinook form? Its creation requires a mountain range that runs perpendicular to the prevailing winds. As the winds blow inland from the coast, they rise to climb over the mountain summits. With increased altitude the temperature drops, and before long, clouds become saturated as the moisture within condenses. These wet clouds cool as they rise, and release their moisture as rain and snow along the western slopes of the Rocky Mountains. By the time they crest the summit of the Continental Divide, they are largely devoid of moisture, and rapidly descend the eastern slopes. Dry air changes temperature with decreasing altitude at almost twice the rate of saturated air. Simply stated, it warms up more coming down the Alberta side than it cools climbing up the western slopes. The end result is a warm, dry wind blowing off the mountains.

What to Wear?

IN THE MOUNTAINS, having the proper clothing can make the difference between a pleasant experience and misery. This is the land of the synthetics. Products like polypropylene and fleece rule the roost. Unlike cotton, which holds moisture and keeps you cold, these materials cannot absorb water, and will continue to keep you warm even when wet.

The motto "Be Prepared" provides words to live by. With weather changing in minutes, having extra clothes to put on, or rain gear to stay dry, can be critical. It can still rain, even on a cloudless day. During winter outings, having warm clothes can be a life saver, especially in the case of unexpected injury.

Dressing in layers allows you to add layers as you cool down, and remove them as you warm up. Heavy layers cause you to sweat as you begin working, and sweating is never good during winter. Suddenly your clothes are wet, and their insulating capacity compromised, especially if you're wearing a cotton T-shirt.

Western anemone

Yarrow

Yellow hedysarum

Cow parsnip

Bunchberry

Plants

In mountainous areas, plants must adapt to the harsh environment in order to survive. Large variations in temperature over a short period of time, mixed with short growing seasons, means only the most versatile plants are found in the mountains.

Many things may determine whether a plant is able to survive in a particular area. In terms of nutrients, if even one critical component is in short supply, the distribution of the plant may be curtailed. A plant's survival is also dependent on less predictable factors. If a particular animal takes a liking to a plant, this may limit its distribution, though the plant may otherwise thrive. Fire may also affect distribution. Other limiting factors include altitude, exposure to sun, temperature, moisture, and wind. If successful, the end result is a delicate, yet vibrant community of plants that are well-adapted to their environment.

Wildflowers
White Flowers

Western Anemone (*Anemone occidentalis*)
Often the first flower to bloom in the alpine, it has five whitish petals and a fuzzy stem and leaves. The flower quickly gives way to a shaggy seed head, earning it the nickname "hippie on a stick."

Yarrow (*Achillea millefolium*)
This umbrella-like flower is widely distributed across Canada. The leaves are finely dissected and look almost fern-like. This plant was used to heal Achilles' soldiers during the Battle of Troy in Greek mythology.

Yellow Hedysarum (*Hedysarum sulphurescens*)
A favourite food of grizzlies, this member of the pea plant is common in spring and early summer. The distinctive pea-like flower heads tend to grow on one side of the tall stem. The leaves grow in groups of 9–17 leaflets, forming a typical compound leaf.

Cow Parsnip (*Heracleum lanatum*)
This giant of a plant may be

Early yellow locoweed

Yellow mountain avens

Shrubby cinquefoil

Brown-eyed Susan

upward of 2 m (7 ft.) in height. Its large umbrella-shaped flower head and huge rhubarb-like leaves make it unmistakable. Another favourite of grizzlies, it is common along moist avalanche slopes. It may also be found along rivers and other wet areas.

Bunchberry *(Cornus canadensis)*
Part of the dogwood family, bunchberry gets its name from the clump of red berries it produces each year. The leaves consist of a rosette of 4–6 leaves. The veins in the leaves clearly run parallel to the outer margin of the leaf, in typical dogwood style. Four whitish bracts that appear as petals form what most people view as the flower.

Yellow Flowers

Early Yellow Locoweed *(Oxytropus sericea)*
Locoweed, like other members of the pea family, is easy to identify. The compound leaves and flower head grow from a common base. The flower is a cream colour, forming a clump of pea-like flowers at the top of a hairy stem. It is poisonous to cattle, and earned its name from its effect on unwary cows.

Yellow Mountain Avens *(Dryas drummondii)*
One of the toughest mountain plants, it forms a carpet along river washes, roadsides, and other inhospitable, dry spots. It has serrated leaves set off by small, nodding yellow flowers. The seed stage resembles a blond ponytail, which opens to form a fluffy seed head.

Shrubby Cinquefoil *(Potentilla fruticosa)*
This common shrub grows as both an ornamental and native plant. Usually a few feet high, it has leaves that grow in groups of 3–7 (usually 5). The flowers are yellow, with five petals, and resemble a buttercup in appearance.

Brown-eyed Susan *(Gaillardia aristata)*
These yellow daisy-like flowers have a chocolate-coloured centre. They are common in the foothills, and their long stalks (30–80 cm, or 12–32 in.) sway in the breeze. The leaves at the base are long and thin, but become heavily toothed along the stem.

Heartleaf arnica

19

Indian paintbrush

Common vetch

Pink wintergreen

Calypso orchid or fairy slipper

Common fireweed

Heartleaf Arnica *(Arnica cordifolia)*

Looking like a yellow daisy, the heartleaf arnica is one of the easiest flowers to identify, and one of the more common. Its green leaves are serrated and heart-shaped. They are also quite large. The flower is common in lodgepole pine forests, and brightens the sparse vegetation.

Pink and Red Flowers

Indian Paintbrush *(Castilleja miniata)*

This versatile flower can vary dramatically in colour, from deep purple to red, yellow or white. The "petals" are really a series of coloured bracts surrounding the small tubular flowers. The top of the plant looks like it has been dipped in paint, hence the name.

Common Vetch *(Vicia americana)*

This trailing vine is common in the lower montane forest. Typical of pea plants, the leaves are in pairs and the flowers are purple in colour. Unlike the Hedysarum, it doesn't stand tall, but uses other plants as an anchor.

Pink Wintergreen *(Pyrola asarifolia)*

This pleasant pink flower is common in lodgepole pine forests during the spring. Waxy in nature, it has a basal rosette of dark leaves. The reddish and cup-shaped flower rises above. The flower is unique and easy to identify.

Calypso Orchid or Fairy Slipper *(Calypso bulbosa)*

This pleasant orchid also brightens up a lodgepole pine forest during June. Unmistakable, this delicate, lady-slipper orchid has pinkish petals above and a large scoop-like lip below—the slipper. There is usually a single basal leaf with the veins running parallel to the leaf margin.

Common Fireweed *(Epilobium angustifolium)*

Often the first flower to colonize a fire site, this plant is aptly named. Forming large fields of pink, its tall stem can be upwards of 2 m (7 ft.) in height. The stem has narrow green leaves growing along it, until it gives way to a pink spike of flowers on the upper portion of the stem.

Shooting star

Prairie crocus or pasque flower

Alpine forget-me-not

Shooting Star *(Dodecatheon radicatum)*

This nodding flower easily lives up to its name. Its reverse petals point upward like the tail of a shooting star, and the flower points toward the ground. The light-green, oblong leaves form a simple rosette at the base of this wonderful flower.

Purple Blue Flowers

Prairie Crocus or Pasque Flower *(Anemone patens)*

This harbinger of spring is a welcome sign each year. Its densely hairy stem hosts a six-petal, purple flower, even before the leaves fully develop. The feathery seed stalk that soon replaces the purple head is also a common sight. It is the provincial flower of Manitoba.

Alpine Forget-me-not *(Myosotis alpestris)*

High in the alpine, the forget-me-not really is unforgettable. Often growing amidst rugged scree slopes, its five blue petals and yellow centre eye are easily identified. The leaves are lance-shaped, covered with soft hairs, and alternate along the length of the stem. The forget-me-not rarely grows more than 20 cm (8 in.) high.

Common Harebell *(Campanula rotundifolia)*

The harebell, also known as the bluebell, is one of the most common flowers. The bell-shaped flowers have five petals and form a cup-like bell. Some are nodding in nature, and the stem may be 15–40 cm (6–16 in.) tall. The leaves are generally basal in nature and somewhat round.

Early Blue Violet *(Viola adunca)*

Another sign of spring, the early blue violet is a pleasant, if tiny, flower. It rarely grows above 10 cm (4 in.) high. The leaves are heart- or kidney-shaped, and the flower distinctive in its appearance.

Animals

Kananaskis Country hosts a diversity of wildlife. Unlike Banff, its boundaries incorporate the transition from plains to foothills to mountains, and contains, therefore, animals and birds from many different habitats.

Viewing wildlife requires the proper mix of knowledge

Common harebell

Early blue violet

Golden eagle

Red-tailed hawk

Red-naped sapsucker

Black-billed magpie

Canada jay

and luck. I've spoken to people that have visited the Kananaskis once and seen cougars. I've spent 10 years in the area and never had such good fortune. On the other hand, the fact animals are not leaping out from behind every tree has a lot to do with our excitement in being treated to a rare sighting. In places like Banff, where elk are sometimes as prevalent as the cameras surrounding them, it doesn't take long before visitors become jaded. This has never been a problem in Kananaskis. With hunting still a part of the annual cycle, the animals have a healthy fear of man, and tend to keep their distance.

The best way to improve your odds is to learn as much as you can about the area's animals—their habitats, diets, and annual cycles. Often, finding the signs of animals—their droppings, markings or nests—can be as enjoyable as spotting the real thing. Sure, nothing beats seeing a bear from the safety of your vehicle, but finding a tree that has been climbed by a black bear,

or the berry-blackened droppings of a grizzly, can also get the blood flowing.

This section will help you identify some of the common birds and animals within Kananaskis Country. It is by no means a definitive list, but is meant to get you started in your Kananaskis wildlife hunt.

Common Wildlife
Birds
Golden Eagle
This relatively common eagle is easily identified by its large size and dark profile. The bald eagle, also fairly common, has a white head and tail. Recently, a migration route for golden eagles was discovered in the Kananaskis area. It nests in the area, and may be seen soaring overhead.
Red-tailed Hawk
Our most common large hawk, the red tail is the key feature for identifying this aerial hunter. It is often seen soaring above open areas looking for ground squirrels. It is also commonly seen perched atop fence posts. The distinctive call is a long whistle.

Raven

Mountain chickadee

Red-breasted nuthatch

Mountain bluebird

Cedar waxwing

Red-naped Sapsucker

This common woodpecker can be identified by its black and white back, buff breast, and red throat and head patches. It also has two white stripes, one above and one below the eye. Like most woodpeckers, it is usually heard pecking before it's observed. It makes parallel rows of holes in trees, and then returns later to eat the insects and sap that has collected.

Black-billed Magpie

This common member of the jay family is notable for its long tail and iridescent colours. It has a black head and beak, with white patches on the side and breast. The tail and lower wings seem to vary from a green to a bluish tint. No other bird has a similarly long tail.

Canada Jay

This common jay is variously known as Gray Jay, Camp Robber, or Whiskey Jack. It is gray in colour, with a short beak and dark patch on the top of the head. Its short beak distinguishes it from the Clark's Nutcracker, for whom it is often mistaken.

Raven

The raven has been maligned through the ages. It is a very large scavenger and our largest songbird. Its heavy beak, large size, and wedge-shaped tail distinguish it from the common crow. Its call is a hoarse croak.

Black-capped Chickadee

The distinctive call of the chickadee, "chick-a-dee-dee-dee," gives this bird its name. Common throughout the area, it has an easily recognized black cap and throat patch. Its breast is buff-coloured. There are two other chickadees in the area: the Boreal Chickadee has a brown cap, and the Mountain Chickadee has a white eye stripe.

Red-breasted Nuthatch

This wonderful bird is another common visitor throughout the area. It has a bluish back and a distinctive rust-coloured breast. It also has a black cap on its head and a white eye stripe. It generally moves down a tree, collecting insects from behind the bark.

Mule deer

Elk

Moose

Bighorn sheep

Mountain goat

Mountain Bluebird

Almost wiped out by competition from introduced cavity nesters like the starling, the mountain bluebird has made a comeback with the help of a large program of nestboxes. It is easily identified as the only bird in the area that is entirely blue in colour. The males are dark blue above, and lighter below. The females are more gray than blue, helping them blend into their surroundings.

Other common birds

- Mallard
- Spruce, Blue, and Ruffed Grouse
- Common Snipe
- Great Horned Owl
- American Dipper
- Nighthawk
- Tree, Cliff, and Barn Swallows
- Clark's Nutcracker
- Bohemian and Cedar Waxwings
- Brown-headed Cowbird
- Dark-eyed Junco

Mammals

The elusive cougar, the ferocious grizzly, the proud mountain goat: these are what people think of when they think of the mountains. The large game provide the impetus for many people to head out onto the backroads and away from the crowds. While Banff is more famous for its wildlife, Kananaskis has the same selection, with some added benefits. Watching a bighorn sheep begging for handouts along the highway may be a novelty, but it's hardly "wild" life. In Kananaskis, when you see a stag elk, you can see the fire in his eye and feel the wildness in his heart. This makes even a common sighting exciting.

Dawn and dusk are your best opportunities for spotting animals. Most animals are more active at these times, and also more visible. While you travel through Kananaskis Country, keep your eyes open for the large animals, but don't forget the smaller, less sensational residents. Animals like the pika can add as much excitement to a child's visit as a grizzly.

Ungulates

Mule Deer

This is our true mountain deer. It is easily identified by

Grizzly bear

Black bear

Cougar

its large mule-like ears, and its black-tipped tail. In the male, the antlers form Y-shaped junctions. It weighs in at about 100 kg (220 lbs.), and stands 100 cm (3 ft.) at the shoulders. It is a browser, eating mainly grasses and flowers, moving on to leaves as the flowers disappear in the latter part of the season. During winter it chews on buds and twigs.

White-tailed Deer

More common in the eastern portions of Kananaskis, the white-tailed deer is a low-elevation animal. Unlike the mule deer, which is common in the mountains, the white-tail tends to be seen along the foothills and plains. It is becoming increasingly popular, in particular along the Bow Valley. It has a brown tail, and when it senses danger, it lifts its tail, revealing the white underside. This flagging warns others of potential harm, and they head for cover. Lighter than the mule deer, it weighs in at about 90 kg (200 lbs.), but stands about the same height at the shoulder.

Elk

These dark, stocky animals are one of the premier game animals in the mountains. The Shawnee Indians called it "Wapiti," which literally translates to "white rump." This is an apt description, as the rump is indeed white, whereas the rest of the animal is brown, the head and shoulders being significantly darker. Elk are heavier than deer, and weigh about 315 kg (694 lbs.). The antlers of the stags can be as long as 150 cm (5 ft.).

Moose

This is the largest member of the deer family. Its large size, dark colour, and magnificent antlers make it distinctive. It weighs about 450 kg (992 lbs.), and its height averages 180 cm (6 ft.) at the shoulder. The word "moose" means "twig eater" in the Algonkian language, and that is exactly what it does. In winter, it browses on the twigs and branches of willows and other local species. In spring, it is often seen feeding in deep marshes.

Bighorn Sheep

Bighorn sheep are often confused with mountain goats. This is largely because the females have short goat-like horns. Only the males get the full curl horns that are so distinctive of this animal. In Kananaskis, if it's not snow-white in colour, it's a sheep. It is common on grassy hillsides, where it feeds, but may come down to the roadsides to lick mineral-rich gravels. It weighs about 125 kg (275 lbs.), and is just under 100 cm (3 ft.) tall at the shoulders.

Mountain Goat

This white goat is not really a goat at all. It is more closely re-

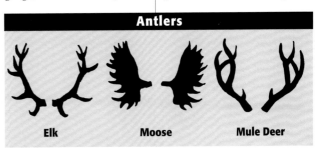

Antlers

Elk

Moose

Mule Deer

Gray wolf

Porcupine

Red squirrel

lated to the mountain antelopes of Asia. Its white coat and dark horns are distinctive. It weighs about 85 kg (187 lbs.), and stands just over 100 cm (3 ft.) at the shoulder. It prefers the true high country, and rarely appears along the roadsides within Kananaskis Country.

Bears
Grizzly Bear
The grizzly seems to epitomize the wilderness. It is large, powerful, and potentially dangerous. It weighs 250–350 kg (550–770 lbs.), and it averages 130 cm (4 ft.), at the shoulders. It has a prominent hump on the shoulders, and a "dished-in" appearance to the face. The claws can be up to 7.5 cm (3 in.) in length, and leave distinctive marks in the footprints.

Black Bear
Our most common bear, the black bear is easily identified by its lack of a shoulder hump, and its dog-like face. It may be black, but it can also be cinnamon-coloured. It tends to weigh about 170 kg (375 lbs.) and stand 95 cm (3 ft.) at the shoulders.

Other predators
Cougar
Rarely seen, the cougar is the largest cat in Kananaskis. It may weigh 70 kg (154 lbs.), and be 150 cm (5 ft.) long (not counting the tail). It hunts the area's large game animals, like moose, elk, deer, and bighorn sheep. After eating their fill, cougars cover the remainder of their prey with leaves and other material, and return later.

Gray Wolf
The wolf is finally returning to the mountains. Wolf studies in Banff National Park show a strong and growing population. It is occasionally seen along roadways, crossing to move to new territories. It weighs about 50 kg (110 lbs.), and varies in colour from gray to almost black.

Other small animals
Porcupine
This prickly rodent is easily recognized by its long hair-like spines. Often its handiwork—plywood signs chewed to splinters or pack straps munched for the salt in the hiker's sweat—makes it less than welcome. It is fairly com-

mon in the Kananaskis area, and is an agile climber. It weighs an average of 6.5 kg (14 lbs.), and measures about 77 cm (3 ft.) long.

Red Squirrel
This noisy resident needs little introduction. With its distinctive reddish colour and bushy tail, it is known far and wide. It forms the early warning system in the forest, announcing your presence to the other forest dwellers. It spends the summers collecting cones, and then stores them to provide a winter food supply. It creates large piles of cone fragments, called middens, and nests beneath them.

Columbian Ground Squirrel
Incorrectly called "gophers," the Columbian ground squirrel is our most common underground resident. Its coat has a "salt-and-pepper" appearance to it, and this is offset by a reddish belly. It lives in large colonies, and you'll often see it standing tall, performing sentry duty. It falls prey to eagles and hawks, and grizzlies like to dig up colonies for a protein fix.

Columbian ground squirrel

Golden-mantled ground squirrel

Pika

Golden-mantled Ground Squirrel

As you climb above the valley bottom, the golden-mantled ground squirrel becomes common. It is similar to, but larger than, a chipmunk, and the stripes stop at the shoulder. On a chipmunk, the stripes continue through the eyes.

They quickly become "spoiled," and end up begging for handouts at viewpoints and attractions. Please don't give in. Let them find their own natural foods.

Pika

The rock rabbit, as the pika is also known, is more closely related to rabbits than rodents.

It lives high in the mountains, usually above 2,000 m (6,560 ft.), and prefers the barren landscape of loose-boulder slopes. It uses the rocks as sentry posts, and the spaces between the rocks as tunnels.

Trees

Trembling Aspen
- small paddle-shaped leaves, long leaf stalk
- most common leafed tree
- bark greenish-white, becoming furrowed with age

Lodgepole Pine
- needles 2.5–7 cm (1–3 in.) long, in groups of two
- cones hard and waxy
- few branches on the lower trunk

White Spruce
- needles square in shape, not in pairs
- cones 5 cm (2 in.) long, and stiff
- often grows under lodgepole pine

Subalpine Fir
- flat needles 2.5–4.5 cm (1–2 in.)
- bark may be smooth with resin blisters
- usually grows above elevations of 1,540 m (5,082 ft.)

Alpine Larch
- soft needles, in groups of 30–40
- loses its needles every year
- oval cones 3–5 cm (1–2 in.) in length

Ecology

In any environment, the interaction between a diverse set of landscapes, varying climatic conditions, and plants and animals makes for unique, yet delicate ecosystems. The study of ecology looks at the whole—the connection between the parts. The more we understand about the landscapes of the Rockies, the more we realize that the rocks are as important as any of the other components making up this diverse ecosystem.

Within Kananaskis Country, each ecological community is known as an ecoregion. These have unique collections of plants and animals adapted to a specific set of geological and climatic conditions. Kananaskis Country includes numerous ecoregions. In the lower valley we find the Mon-

tane. Further to the east, on the edge of plain and foothill, lies the Aspen Parkland.

The parkland is characterized by forests of trembling aspen mixed with open grassland. Warm, south-facing slopes are often devoid of trees, and cooler, wetter, north-facing slopes are darkened by white spruce. Animals like the coyote, white-tailed deer, elk, and ruffed grouse call the parkland home.

As you move westward, the altitude increases and the Montane forest becomes dominant. This forest community is characterized by Douglas fir and limber pine. Often the lower slopes of the Rockies are improperly identified as Montane when they are actually Boreal Foothills, or Boreal Uplands. Douglas fir and limber pine thrive in the dry, Chi-

nook-blasted valleys of the lower eastern slopes. Located between 1,200 (3,960) and 1,500–1,650 m (4,950–5,445 ft.), the Montane forest comprises most of the valley of the Bow River, as well as parts of the Elbow and Sheep river valleys. This is prime elk habitat, along with white-tailed and mule deer, black bear, spruce grouse, and snowshoe hare.

More common than the Montane is the Boreal Foothills ecoregion. Typically comprising dense forests of lodgepole pine, white spruce, trembling aspen, and balsam poplar, it is the third-largest ecoregion in the province. The Boreal Foothills begins at approximately 1,340 m (4,422 ft.), and may be interspersed with various Montane species. With increasing altitude, it gives way to the Boreal Uplands.

This is identified by a notice-able lack of aspen and poplar, and normally borders the sub-alpine, at approximately 1,540 m (5,082 ft.). Common wildlife include ruffed grouse, snow-shoe hare, lynx, black bear, and white-tailed and mule deer.

The Subalpine is a zone of transition. It begins as the trees of the Montane and Bo-real Uplands give way to sub-alpine fir and Engelmann spruce. Alpine larch may also be present in this zone. Climb-ing upwards through the sub-alpine, the trees get progres-sively more stunted in appear-ance, until they exhibit a growth form known as "krummholz." German for "crooked wood," krummholz are small clumps of stunted trees that provide protection for each other. Often only a metre (a few feet tall), the trees may be several hundred years old. Eventually, by approxi-mately 2,300 m (7,590 ft.), the trees begin to disappear, and we enter the true Alpine. Like its plant community, the ani-mals of the subalpine tend to be a mixture of those prefer-ring higher or lower locales. You may see a ptarmigan pick-ing at willow buds or a red squirrel scurrying through the trees. Animals like the marten prefer the dense forests, while bighorn sheep prefer the open slopes near the margin of alpine and subalpine.

The alpine is a rugged place. It's an area where even the toughest trees cannot sur-vive. Biologists studying tree-lines have found that the cut-off for most species will occur at the point where the average July temperature is 10°C (50°F). This tends to hold true from Alaska to California. With the lack of tree growth, the alpine blooms in July and sup-ports plants capable of living in harsh climates. Low-lying flowers, many of which repro-duce vegetatively due to the short growing season, make up the majority of the plant life in the alpine. Animals like the mountain goat, the tiny pika, and the ptarmigan make the alpine their home. They have learned to prosper where other animals may have floun-dered. For some alpine ani-mals, the unique collection of hardy plants mixed with the high winds, have combined to create a wind-blown world where forage is available year round. In the open habitats, grizzly bears and bighorn sheep forage, while the pika rules the rocks.

Above: Barrier Lake and Mount Lorette

29

Multiple-use in Theory and Practice

Kananaskis Country is like few other areas in the world. From its earliest inception, it was designed to accommodate a multitude of users and support limited resource extraction while still maintaining traditional uses such as grazing. This was an intimidating task, but it began long before the official designation of Kananaskis Country.

Around the turn of the century, the eastern slopes of the Rocky Mountains began seeing increasing pressure on their resources. Ranchers had moved cattle up the valleys of the foothills, forests were falling under the axe, rivers were being diverted for irrigation, and coal was being mined in numerous areas. The government realized that a program of controlled conservation would be necessary to ensure the future of this area. Even though Alberta gained provincial status in 1905, the federal government maintained control on the province's natural resources

until 1930.

In 1906 the Forest Reserve Act placed restriction on the sale of most of the eastern slopes. This prohibited homesteading, and numerous settlers were moved out of the area. There were provisions in the act to allow mining, logging, resource extraction, and limited grazing. During this period, the forest rangers were responsible for the management of the forest reserves, as well as all the fish and game in the area.

In 1911 the Forest Reserve Act was supplemented with the Dominion Forest Reserves and Parks Act. This controlled logging through the issuance of permits.

With increased ranching pressure, a permit system was implemented in 1914. This promoted the forming of cattle associations, and grazing was limited to specific allotments, thus initiating the system of grazing-distribution units still used today. Range inventories over the years

have provided data on carrying capacities, and this has been used in the issuance of permits.

In 1930 the Alberta government took control of its natural resources for the first time. The Alberta Department of Lands and Mines assumed control, and was subdivided into five branches: Forestry, Mines, Lands, Fisheries, and Water Power. Unfortunately the Alberta government gained control just as the Great Depression set in. This was followed by several years of extensive forest fires. By the early 1940s, the provincial government was feeling the strain, and in 1947 a joint federal-provincial body was organized to take over management of the eastern slopes.

The Eastern Rockies Forest Conservation Board (ERFCB) had a 25-year mandate, and immediately passed the Eastern Rockies Forest Conservation Act. Their mandate included the construction of facilities, the protection of forests, and the conservation, maintenance, and development of the forest resources, all with a focus on water flow management.

The capital period, between 1947 and 1955, saw a flurry of development. Facilities were upgraded, new roads built, and equipment modernized. It was during this period that the forestry trunk road from Nordegg to Coleman was built. This includes present-day Highway 40.

The ERFCB also set about to collect watershed and climatic data on the area, and began recording temperature, wind, humidity, and cloud-cover information. This was done in conjunction with stream-flow gauges to measure and predict river flows. This research helped them to modify and update the grazing allotment system within the foothills.

When the mandate of the ERFCB expired in 1968, it

acted as an advisory council until it was disbanded in 1973. The Alberta Forest Service (AFS) once again took control of the province's wilderness. The AFS continued many of the programs initiated by the ERFCB.

In 1977 the Alberta government published "A Policy for Resource Management of the Eastern Slopes." This document used the concept of carrying capacity as a basis for zoning on the eastern slopes. Areas were zoned based on the types of impact they could sustain.

Also in 1977, Kananaskis Country was officially announced, and began its own period of capital development. For the next 15 years, tens of millions of dollars were spent on the upgrading of roads and campgrounds, the building of a golf course, Olympic ski hill and cross-country ski site, the development of a hotel complex, and numerous other projects.

In 1983, when Kananaskis

Country announced its "Kananaskis Resource Management Policy," it followed the recommendations of the 1977 Eastern Slopes Policies. Since then, it has provided resource protection, while still attempting to provide facilities for as wide a variety of users as possible. There are 4x4 and snowmobile areas, some oil and gas exploration, and limited logging, as well as hiking, biking, horseback riding, hunting, and fishing. This list is by no means exhaustive.

Kananaskis Country is always undergoing change. As budgets became increasingly tight, the government moved to a program of privatization and private sector partnerships. Most of the campgrounds have been turned over to private operators, and many other facilities and services may be likewise transferred. Kananaskis changes with the times.

Co Ltd Capt. Stock $ 300.000 160. Acres Close to Dingma
rilling After First Issue of Stock $ 200.000 Shares
Short time only 25¢ per Shar
ue of Stock 25¢ Selling for a
Promotion stock Issue
turday at 9 AM. Obsolutley no
ACME OIL Co Ltd
HEAD OFFICE
SHINE.
ADANAC
OIL CO. LTD

3. Highlights of History

Filling barrels with oil at Discovery Well, Turner Valley, 1914

The Kananaskis has seen many travellers over the years. Beginning with early bands of nomadic hunters, the valley has evolved into an internationally recognized destination. Through its history, Kananaskis Country has reflected the history of southern Alberta. It witnessed the railway surveyors, the origin of ranching, the beginnings of the oil and gas industry, prisoner-of-war camps, and even an Olympics.

11,000 BP – Following a pathway formed by an ice-free corridor between the winding mountain glaciers and the expansive continental ice sheet, small bands of nomadic hunters made their way into the area by following wandering herds of animals. They crossed from Siberia to Alaska along a land bridge formed by lower ocean levels during the ice age. As they passed, they left evidence of their presence.

1787 – Fur trader David Thompson made his first trip into the mountains. Thompson spent his life mapping the west and learning native languages and stories.

1792 – Peter Fiddler entered the foothills and mapped some areas of Kananaskis Country, including the Sheep River.

1800 – David Thompson passed through the area a second time when he travelled past present-day High River on his return from Rocky Mountain House. The next 30 years would not see much white travel in this area, as the Peigan Indians avoided contact with the Hudson's Bay Company.

1841 – James Sinclair of the Hudson's Bay Company passed present-day Canmore, continuing through the Spray Valley on his way to the newly opened Oregon territory. He was taking Scottish settlers from the Red River Settlement, then located near present-day Winnipeg.

1845 – Father Jean de Smet passed by present-day Canmore on his way east from British Columbia

1854 – James Sinclair was sent by George Simpson to take a second group of British settlers to the Oregon territory. They brought along with them

250 horses and oxen, 15 white families, and approximately 100 Cree to protect the group from possible Blackfoot attacks. This time, he travelled via the Kananaskis valley.

1858 – The British and Canadian Governments sent John Palliser to undertake the first in-depth surveys of what is now Western Canada.

1860s – The life of the plains Indian began to change rapidly as the bison began to disappear and whiskey traders began to test the waters of southern Alberta.

In the late 1960s, a man known as One Spot Samples opened a short-lived Whiskey Fort on the Sheep River. He probably only operated one season before clearing out.

1870 – The Hudson's Bay Company relinquished its control over its vast western land holdings. Suddenly the west was without formal pro-

Eau Claire and Bow River Lumber Company logging camp

tection, as the fledgling country of Canada had no official representatives in the wilderness. Whiskey traders quickly moved north from Montana and began to sell whiskey to the local Indians.

Along the Elbow River, two such forts were erected. In 1871, a part-time sheriff from

Montana—Fred Kanouse—opened a post. During his first season, he was lucky to escape with his life after a long siege attempt by the Bloods. Despite this, he did return for a second season of trading.

A second fort trying to compete with him was opened by Dick Berry in 1872. Berry

The Palliser Expedition

DURING THE EARLY to mid-19th century, the Hudson's Bay Company ruled the Canadian west. Very secretive, it allowed little information on the west to make its way back to either Upper Canada or Britain. It realized that information was power, and the Bay Men didn't want to relinquish any of their lands. They worried about settlers scaring away the animals, and that was bad for business. As a result, they kept everything tightly locked away.

John Palliser was commissioned to do the first in-depth surveys of the west and to report his findings back to London. Along with him came Dr. James Hector (physician and geologist),

Eugene Bourgeau (botanist), and Lieutenant Thomas Blakiston (magnetical observer). The group split up to cover more territory and, as a result, each individual was responsible for a variety of discoveries in these different areas.

Palliser travelled into the Kananaskis and bestowed its name. He heard a legend of an Indian by the same name, who apparently had been hit in the head with a battle axe and survived. Since this was a tough valley, and that was one tough Indian, the valley was given his name. His subsequent report on this valley led to the Vermilion Pass being chosen over the Kananaskis Valley as the future

route for a highway.

The expedition completed detailed surveys of most of Alberta, and was the first to describe the valuable coal reserves in this province. It also detailed the prairies, and marked off the famed Palliser Triangle as worthless farmland. Palliser felt the possibility of a railroad remote, and even a wagon road far premature. His expedition was an important part of this areas early non-native history.

Hector also travelled through part of Kananaskis. He followed Swift Water Creek (now the Elbow River), and caught 36 trout in less than two hours.

Prisoners at Kananaskis Valley Internment Camp

was later killed by one of his customers, a Blood Indian.

1881 – George Dawson surveyed the Kananaskis valley between 1881 and 1884, and was later followed-up by his assistant, R.C. McConnell.

1882 – John Ware arrived. He was a former slave who became Alberta's most famous black cowboy. He was also one of the Sheep River valley's first settlers in 1891. His brand "9999" became well known in the area.

1883–84 – The vast forests in the Bow and Kananaskis valleys came under the scrutiny of L.B. Stewart, a Dominion surveyor, who divided the area into timber limits. Soon after, Kutusoff MacFee, along with the Eau Claire and Bow River Lumber Company, began exploiting these deposits. By 1886, their mill in Calgary was producing more than three million board feet annually.

1880s – T.K. Fullerton made numerous attempts to start a timber operation in the Elbow Valley, with little success. Later, around 1905, his son,

T.W. Fullerton, would be successful. The Fullerton's are still a dominant name in the Bragg Creek area today.

1903 – The coal seams of Ribbon Creek were assessed for their commercial value by D.B. Dowling. The results of this assessment were published in 1909, sparking increasing interest in the area's rich deposits.

1914 – Oil was discovered at Turner Valley when Dingman #9 blew out. This same year, a small well near present-day Bragg Creek Provincial Park was opened. The Mowbray–Berkley well was a poor performer and only operated for a few years.

1932–3 – Construction on the hydro projects on the Kananaskis Lakes began. Ten years later, the original dam was replaced, and it was again modified between 1947 and 1955.

1936 – Depression workers built the first road down the Kananaskis Valley. Little more than a narrow cart track, access to the valley remained difficult.

1939 – With war in Europe, the former Relief Camp became an internment camp for German and Italian nationals. This lasted only a short time, until the detainees were released or moved to other camps. The camp was then converted to a prisoner-of-war-camp and used for the duration of hostilities.

1945 – Development of the Barrier Lake Reservoir began with German prisoners-of-war clearing the forests.

1951 – The Spray Lakes Reservoir opened, along with its original power-generating structures.

1952 – The Forestry Trunk Road was opened and passed south through the Kananaskis Valley, all the way to Coleman. This finally allowed easy access to this remote area.

1977 – The Alberta government, under Premier Peter Lougheed, set aside 4,000 sq. km (1,600 sq. mi.) of Alberta's eastern slopes as Kananaskis Country. This mixture of prairie, foothill, and Rocky Mountain includes four Provincial Parks: Bragg Creek, Bow Valley, and Kananaskis (now Peter Lougheed Provincial Park), and the newly established Elbow–Sheep Wildland Park.

4. Life in the Mountains

The Bow Valley from Chinaman's Peak

Kananaskis Country is not a park—it is a recreation area that contains four provincial parks. This structure allows it to support more varied recreational pursuits than the vast majority of "parks." Through its multiple-use mandate, it accommodates many types of users, but keeps them separate whenever possible. For instance, the McLean Creek Off-Highway Vehicle Zone provides a large area specifically for dirt bikes, four-wheel-drive vehicles, and, in winter, snowmobiles. Since these activities are incompatible with hiking, the facilities have been separated from non-motorized recreation. In the past, many of the routes followed by today's hiking trails were open to off-highway traffic. The Big Elbow, Little Elbow, and Sheep trails are examples of former vehicle-access roads that have been converted to non-motorized use only. Although the closure of these areas to vehicles was controversial, the provision of high-quality facilities elsewhere helped to ease the change.

Since Kananaskis Country's inception, an almost limitless number of facilities, campgrounds, and trails have been created to facilitate increased access to the area. Today there are thousands of campsites, along with hundreds of kilometres of trails. Dirt bikes are able to coexist with horseback riders. Mountain bikers maintain a relatively peaceful relationship with horse and hiking traffic. Kananaskis is more than a few highways providing access to magnificent scenery—it's a place to play!

Frontcountry Camping

Perhaps more than any other activity, camping is something that brings families into the area and allows them to become intimate with the many riches that Kananaskis has to offer. Most of the campgrounds offer basic services, including drinkable water, washroom facilities, firepits, and picnic tables. A few sites require you to boil water before using, but they tend to be remote areas, and the water

Opposite: Cycling the Evan–Thomas bicycle path

sources are posted unsafe for drinking.

Camping in western Kananaskis is extremely popular. You'll travel Highway 40 for 23 km (13.8 mi.) before encountering your first campground. Uniquely designed, Sundance Lodges offers a completely different camping experience. Instead of tents or camper trailers, you can stay in an authentic Sioux-designed, hand-painted teepee. Also included are hot showers, washrooms, coin laundry, pay phone, and small grocery store. Facilities for traditional trailers and tents are also available—some of them adjacent to teepees. Reservations can be made by calling (403) 591-7122.

Mount Kidd R.V. Park provides deluxe camping, with everything you could ever want. Just a few minutes from the Kananaskis Golf Course, it includes such options as electricity, satellite TV, laundry facilities, showers, flush toilets, snack bar, convenience store, games room, sauna, and Jacuzzi tub. Reservations are essential for this perpetually busy campsite. Call (403) 591-7700 to ensure a site for your stay.

Farther south, within Peter Lougheed Provincial Park, there are seven campgrounds, designed to accommodate more traditional camping. There are no satellite hookups, in fact no electrical hookups at all. What they do offer is location! The 16 km (10 mi.) Kananaskis Lakes Trail accesses some of the area's premier hiking, mountain biking, cross-country skiing, and fishing. Of the six campsites, the

Mount Kidd R.V. Park

most popular are Boulton and Elkwood. These two offer the advantage of showers, as well as amphitheatres for interpretive programs. Boulton also has a small store and restaurant.

Beyond the junction to the Kananaskis Lakes, the campgrounds are much more primitive. There are no summer campsites until beyond Highwood Junction. However, during the hunting season, Strawberry campground, just north of the Junction, is opened. South of the Junction, Etherington and Cataract Creek campgrounds offer basic services only.

Along the Trans Canada Highway, in Bow Valley

What to Bring

CAMPING IS THE sort of activity that takes you far from the luxury of home and makes you choose those items that you simply can't live without. It's amazing to see the choices made by some campers—hairdryers make their way to campgrounds without electrical hookups. It's important to keep in mind certain items that should be included in any camper's list of essentials. Here is a list of suggested supplies:

- flashlight with extra batteries
- barbecue or Coleman stove
- matches—lots of them
- camera, film, and extra

batteries
- tent if not travelling with a larger unit
- tarp to shelter picnic table
- at least one complete change of clothes, including shoes
- warm jacket for the evening
- hat and gloves, even in summer
- rain gear
- good footwear
- axe—not a hatchet
- toiletries and towel
- first aid kit
- mosquito repellent
- sunscreen

Mount Glasgow from Nihahi Creek Trail

Provincial Park, Bow Valley Campground provides basic services, whereas Willow Rock offers the advantage of electrical hookups on some sites. Some sites at Bow Valley Campground can be reserved by calling (403) 673-2163. In addition to basic services, both offer showers, a dumping station, and a playground. Two other campgrounds, Lac Des Arcs and Bow River, are located along the Trans Canada Highway, and offer basic services only.

Sibbald Creek Trail provides more rustic accommodation. Sibbald Lake Campground provides basic ser-

vices, while Dawson Equestrian, at the head of the dusty Powderface Trail, provides limited facilities for those camping with their horses.

The Elbow Valley is less hectic, yet it provides numerous camping opportunities. It has five campgrounds along Highway 66, and two farther south, at the end of McLean Creek Trail. All provide basic facilities, with McLean Creek, Paddy's Flat, and the Little Elbow adding amphitheatres for evening naturalist shows. McLean Creek offers some sites for off-highway vehicle users, while the Little Elbow offers corrals for horses. Some sites at McLean Creek and Little Elbow campgrounds can be reserved by calling (403) 949-3132.

Last, but not least, the Sheep River Valley, west of Turner Valley, provides two basic campgrounds: Sandy McNabb and Bluerock. Both have traditional and equestrian camping, and provide only basic facilities.

Backcountry Camping

For those hikers that prefer the solitude of the backcountry, Kananaskis provides numerous opportunities to explore, and you will still enjoy the luxury of a well-designed campground. In the past, backcountry campers chose their own sites, and tented wherever the spirit moved them. Today, with increasing numbers of people heading into the wilderness, this practice leads to excessive impact and unnecessary hardship. Kananaskis Country has developed backcountry campsites designed to assist you in tak-

Summer Theatre

KANANASKIS COUNTRY is famous for its interpretive theatre programs. They run throughout the summer in many of the campgrounds, and are designed to provide an entertaining way to learn about the area's natural and human history. These programs include traditional nature hikes, as well as entertaining evening amphitheatre programs. During these plays, comedy is used to help ease the educational message. If the audience is laughing at a clever presentation, they may not realize they are learning something. It also helps keep the kids atten-

The stage is set

tion for the length of the program.

The programs in Kananaskis have become a yardstick against which similar programs elsewhere are compared. Stop in at any of the visitor centres for information on summer programming.

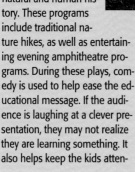

World-famous Golf

Kananaskis Country Golf Course—fast becoming famous

SITTING BENEATH THE imposing slopes of Mount Kidd, and along the winding course of the Kananaskis River, the Kananaskis Golf Course provides one of the most dramatic golf courses in North America. Its 36 holes will challenge even the most accomplished player.

The course was designed by Robert Trent Jones, a man famous for designing difficult, but spectacular, courses. With over 400 courses to his credit, Jones picked the location after flying over the valley in a helicopter. He described the site as, "The finest location I have ever seen for a golf course." Into his design he integrated white sands imported from British Columbia, along with vast amounts of water, extensive fairways, and undulating greens.

When it comes to sand, this course spared no expense. In order to provide the best sand possible, $345,000 was spent importing large-particle white silica from Golden, B.C. The silica was almost double the cost of regular sand, but had several benefits that justified its cost. Primary among these was a large grain size, which makes it heavy and resistant to the high winds in the valley. The silica, unlike sand, has a tendency to remain fluffy, rather than to pack down like normal sand, and, visually, the white colour of the silica complements the glacial landscapes of the Rockies.

ing advantage of the wilderness, while still providing a little comfort. In keeping with this philosophy, they discourage random camping. These backcountry sites provide the convenience of a privy toilet, fire pits, moderately level sites, and a place to hang your food.

Most of the backcountry sites along the Kananaskis valley are designed for backpackers. Most of the campsites are along hiking-only trails, which means they are great for those people that prefer a quieter experience. Elbow Lake campsite, west of Highway 40, is the only one in Peter Lougheed Provincial Park that allows horse access. It is also accessible by mountain bike.

Several of the campgrounds provide loop options, in particular the campsites of Ribbon Falls, Ribbon Lake, and Lillian Lake. This loop can keep the backcountry fishermen busy for several days, as these regularly stocked lakes challenge your skills. The loop is easiest in the order listed above, as a rock wall above Ribbon Falls is easier to negotiate in the uphill direction.

Within Peter Lougheed Provincial Park's facility zone, there are four backcountry sites: Point, Forks, Three Isle Lake, and Turbine Canyon. They're all located west of the Kananaskis Lakes, and provide access towards the north and south Kananaskis passes.

Quaite Valley campground, operated by Bow Valley Provincial Park, is located along the trail of the same name, between Jewell Pass and the Trans Canada Highway.

The eastern portions of Kananaskis Country really shine when it comes to backcountry camping. Part of this lies in the area's popularity with equestrian users, and the system of campsites reflects this. Most are used primarily by horseback campers, and all are in fairly remote areas. They are however, accessible by hikers and bikers as well, adding to their popularity.

Between the Elbow and Sheep River valleys there are numerous sites. These include Big Elbow, Tombstone, and Mount Romulus along the popular Elbow Loop trail system. Spur trails from this provide access to Threepoint Mountain and Wildhorse campgrounds. South of the Sheep River Trail (Highway

Mozart on the Mountain

WHO SAYS SKI HILLS are for skiing only? Nakiska at Mount Allan has found a way to turn their huge alpine amphitheatre into an outdoor concert venue. In this case, the music is classical, and every September the Calgary Philharmonic puts on a spectacular outdoor concert at the base of the Olympic ski hill. Since 1991, this has become an annual event, and the numbers keep rising. In 1995, over 13,000 people showed up, and the Trans Canada Highway, not to mention Highway 40, stopped moving. It took some people 3–4 hours to do the one–hour drive from Calgary. The secret here is to come very early to avoid the crowds. Once you arrive on the site, you can choose from the cramped seating at the base of the hill, or climb a little and leave the

Thousands gather for a little classical music

crowds—not to mention the washrooms—behind. With such success, the Philharmonic, along with Nakiska, have great hopes for this event. 1995 was the 40th anniversary of the Calgary Philharmonic, and they put on an amazing show. Beginning with Aaron Copland's Fanfare for the Common Man, and Mozart's Marriage of Figaro, they slowly built up the momentum. As the program neared its end, they added a medley from the Disney film "The Lion King," and finished with the 1812 Overture as fireworks exploded above the concert site.

Bear Encounters

CAMPING AND HIKING in bear country requires caution and respect. Some people are so concerned about encountering bears that they avoid camping and hiking altogether. The mountains beg to be explored, and bears are an integral part of this wilderness. Without their proud presence, we would all be poorer.

In years of mountain camping, hiking, and biking, you can meet many bears and never have a negative encounter. George Field, one of Kananaskis' Alpine Rescue Specialists, could not recall in 1995 a single bear injury in Kananaskis Country, and he has been involved since 1982. Knowledge is a powerful weapon against fear. By learning about bears, their habits and habitats, you can minimize unwanted encounters on the trail. When camping, a clean site is the best insurance against visits by master bruin. Bears are lazy, they tend to take the most easily available food. If your site is pristine, and someone else has left a cooler out, it's not hard to guess where the bear will head. Avoid bringing anything into the tent that has a strong odour. Bears see better with their nose than their eyes. Don't use sweet-smelling soaps or deodorants, and never bring food or toothpaste into the tent. In Kananaskis, with its bear-proof garbage cans, extensive public

education, and ever vigilant rangers, the problem of campground bears is minimized.

When hiking, make sure the bears know you're coming. Groups of hikers generally make

Black bear

Grizzly bear

noise by talking, and the bear is warned of their approach. Lone hikers need to make a point of making noise. Give out a holler every once and awhile, and don't trust bear bells. They don't make a very loud noise, and tend to create a false sense of security.

The most dangerous situation occurs when the wind is in your face as you pass a loud stream. The bear may not hear or smell you approaching. Make an extra effort to ensure it knows you are

in the area, and be especially vigilant.

If you suddenly find yourself eye to eye with a bear, don't panic. In most cases the bear will defer to your authority and leave without delay. If you are very close, and he feels threatened, he may try a bluff charge. This straight-legged charge is a good time to show him that you are indeed harmless. Move slowly away, don't make any sudden moves, and definitely don't run.

Look around you for any suitable tree to climb, should the situation continue to deteriorate. Although grizzlies can climb trees, they rarely do so. Black bears may follow you up, but normally use the opportunity to retreat.

As a final resort, in a daytime grizzly encounter, you can play dead. In the case of black bears, always fight back. More timid than grizzly bears, they are often easily intimidated. If you do end up playing dead, your pack, if you still have it, can provide some additional protection. Drop to the ground and curl up into a tight ball. Use your hands to protect your neck, and, if possible, pull your pack up to provide some added protection for this vulnerable area. Remember, it is highly unlikely you will ever need to resort to playing dead. The more vigilant we are while hiking, the safer will be our forays into the wilderness.

Cresting one more hill

546), Wolf Creek Campground provides the sole backcountry site.

Hiking

If there's one activity that brings more people to Kananaskis Country than any other, with the exception of sightseeing, it's got to be hiking. There's something magical about getting off the beaten path and wandering along a wilderness trail. Most of the trails are well maintained, and important junctions are signed. The trails run the entire spectrum, from tender strolls to rugged subalpine slogs. With 1,360 km (845 mi.) of trails, there's more than enough to keep the avid hiker busy for season after season. Other trails tend to beckon you back, like an old friend, welcoming you to its varying seasons and moods.

Hiking, like any alpine activity, requires caution and common sense. Many hikers in Kananaskis have problems because they don't plan for contingencies or don't want to carry too much weight. Never head off the highway without a well-stocked daypack, and always plan for the unexpected.

The trails within the Kananaskis area are as diverse as the landscape. Along the main valley, some popular trails include Prairie View, Centennial Ridge, Ribbon Creek, Galatea, and Ptarmigan Cirque. Many offer the hiker panoramic views of the surrounding peaks and valleys, although there is a price—plenty of elevation gain. Others follow the meandering streams towards pleasant lakes and waterfalls.

One hazard within Kananaskis Country relates to the fact that many hiker-defined routes are described in trail guides without specifying their rough character. These are not formally designated hiking routes. There are no signs, maps, or markers of any kind. They require the hiker to be familiar with route-finding and confident in travelling off the beaten path. For this reason, such routes are not described in this book.

Some trails require you to ford streams, which may be high during spring runoff. Fording can be dangerous business. Take the time to move slowly, place each foot firmly before continuing, and use a walking stick, if possible, for balance. Never take a seemingly simple ford for granted. Most accidents occur when we let our guard down. Water is a powerful force and needs to be treated accordingly.

Speaking of water, make sure you bring lots of it with you. With increased travel into the backcountry, the danger of bringing more than the water home with you gets greater. Giardiasis, also known as beaver fever, is becoming more common, and all water sources must be suspect. Avoid drinking from streams. Make sure you boil water for at least five minutes before drinking. Normal chlorine tablets don't kill *Giardia* cysts. Filters need to be capable of filtering organisms measuring as small as .4 microns. To reduce the spread of this malady, make sure you don't void within 50 m (165 ft.) of a water source, and bury all solid wastes.

Another scourge of hikers are wood ticks. These tough little critters are more common during spring, and often find their way into tender areas to steal a blood meal. They are not to be feared, but respected. A good tick check is a necessary addition to any spring hiking activities.

Mountain Biking

Mountain biking is a relative newcomer to the mountain recreation scene. Over the past ten years, the quality of equipment has improved and bikers have extended their reach into more and more remote areas. Kananaskis, with its multiple-use mandate, is one of the few areas that looks at mountain biking as an appropriate activity. With this in mind, the mountain biker in Kananaskis has endless opportunity for excitement.

The Kananaskis valley has numerous trails that are ideal for riding a bike. It is important, however, particularly in this area, that cyclists are courteous and make sure that hikers are aware of their approach. Get off your bike and allow hikers to pass. With increased animosity between hikers and mountain bikers, more and more trails are being closed to cyclists. Some of the trails in the area may be ideal for riding, but their popularity with hikers makes cycling them inappropriate and, in some cases, dangerous.

Within Peter Lougheed Provincial Park there are numerous trails that provide the length that cyclists want and the opportunity to attain some lofty viewpoints. The Kananaskis Fire Lookout is a particularly good example. With clear views high above the Kananaskis Lakes, this trail is worth experiencing. Most of the best cycling routes are used less by hikers due to their long length and, in some cases, lack of scenery. On the other hand, hikers can attain views inaccessible to fat tires.

Further south, into the Highwood area, there are numerous trails radiating out from the highway. Some of these are non-maintained, former fire roads, so be prepared for many natural hazards and obstacles. The main network of signed trails in this area radiates west from the area of Etherington Creek and Cataract Creek campgrounds.

The premier areas for mountain biking within Kananaskis Country are centered around the Sibbald, Elbow, and Sheep river areas. The intensive equestrian use through these corridors has resulted in a well-developed series of trails designed with horses in mind. However, the two activities are not all that different: both try to cover similar distances and both prefer some solid surface on which to ride.

Since mountain bikes can reach far into the wilderness in a very short time, it's important to be prepared for any contingency. Proper repair kits are essential. Some vital inclusions are: spare tube and patch kit, chain tool and extra links, air pump, spoke and Allan wrenches, and the ever

Tips for the Trail

Ah, Hiking! The freedom of the hills…the call of the wild…uh oh, I've got a blister and I've still got 9 km to go. We've all lived it. We begin the day with great intentions, and then some simple oversight, or some not-so-simple oversight, ends up ruining the trip. We crawl back to the trailhead wondering why we put ourselves through such agony. Hiking, like any outdoor pursuit, requires planning and proper technique. There is method to this madness. Here are some hints to help ensure your hike is enjoyable.

- Don't try to go too far, especially on the first hike of the season.
- Keep a steady pace. Too fast or too slow can be tiring, as can an erratic pace.

- When walking uphill, shorten the stride and place your hands on your thighs to help provide a little extra push.
- On the downhill, bend the knees slightly to reduce the strain and constant pounding on these vulnerable joints. This also reduces the likelihood of falling face-first, as it puts your weight a little lower to the ground.
- Good footwear is worth its weight in gold. Don't head out on a long hike with new boots.
- Make sure your first aid kit has plenty of moleskin for treating blisters.
- When loading your daypack, place the heaviest objects close to your back, and high. This places them at the opti-

mum point for hiking, and provides for a more stable load.
- Always bring along extra clothing, rain gear, gloves, and a hat, even on nice days.
- Take time to enjoy the destination. Don't plan a trip that is so ambitious that you're too rushed and can't enjoy the views you've worked so hard to see.

Essential First Aid Kit
Before tossing it in your pack, make sure your first aid kit includes the following essentials:
- plenty of adhesive bandages
- a moleskin and scissors
- gauze pads
- triangular bandages
- a tensor bandage

Taking it all in while riding the Forget-me-not Rounder route

Cross-Country Skiing

Cross-country skiing is one of the fastest growing winter activities, and cross-country skiers seem to be heading into the mountains in increasing numbers. Kananaskis Country has anticipated this increased use, and provides a huge number of properly track-set and maintained cross-country trails. Centered primarily in the western parts of Kananaskis, simply because the eastern valleys don't tend to hold enough snow, these trails can keep you busy for season after season.

Travelling south in the Kananaskis valley, the Ribbon Creek Trail system is the first network encountered. It includes 17 different trails, all ra-

necessary duct tape.

While riding, always ride at a controlled speed. Many accidents are caused by riding too fast. Make sure you stay on designated trails, and avoid riding muddy trails and trampling native vegetation. Make sure you always wear a helmet, and never head out without

letting someone know of your destination. With the ability to cycle in one day what would take a hiker three days, there is a potential for getting caught out overnight. With this in mind, make sure you bring enough extra clothes and food to make it through the night, just in case.

Hiking Trails

diating out of the Ribbon Creek/Kananaskis Village area. You can make your way 5 km (3 mi.) down Ribbon Creek before turning around, or you can climb high above the valley towards Skogan Pass or the Sunburst Lookout. Numerous trails provide loop options out from and around the Kananaskis Village. Another trail of note, the Evan–Thomas Trail, follows the route of the paved summer trail, and trends south from Ribbon Creek all the way to Wedge Pond.

Beyond Ribbon Creek, the Kananaskis Lakes area of Peter Lougheed Provincial Park provides the most popular network of trails. Not only is this network larger than the Ribbon Creek system, but it provides the option of skiing some longer trails. Loops in excess of 30 km (18 mi.) can be created by linking many of the trails together. Some climb toward panoramic viewpoints. In particular, the Kananaskis Fire Lookout, for expert skiers, has the best skiable view in the area. Blueberry Hill provides another good view of the Kananaskis Lakes. Beginner trails, like Pocaterra or Lionel, make sure that skiers of all abilities find something to challenge them.

Along the Smith–Dorrien/Spray Trail, there are two trail systems. The Smith–Dorrien Trail System provides a variety of loop options of varying difficulties. Each loop is colour-coded, and the trail map provides good details on gradients and level. Further north, the Mount Shark Trail system gives racers a place to put in some miles. It is used primar-

Backcountry skiers leave the trails behind

ily for early- and late-season races, when the Canmore Nordic Centre is not at its best.

Designed for the 1988 Winter Olympics, the Canmore Nordic Centre provides an intricate series of trails designed to test the skills of the world's best skiers. The Banff Trail provides the single beginner-trail option. The remainder are one-way racing trails designed for intermediate and expert skiers.

Horseback Riding

Horses have been travelling the trails of Kananaskis for over 100 years. Long before there was a recreational attraction to this valley, ranchers ranged their cattle through its isolated valleys. Range riders kept a constant vigil on the stock, and forest rangers patrolled the valleys.

As time passed, and southern Alberta saw more and more settlement, horses began to take on the dual role of work animal and recreational animal. In time, trails were developed, and today several areas of Kananaskis have been specifically adapted to offer equestrian users the ultimate

in backcountry riding. At present, there are 825 km (513 mi.) of trails within Kananaskis Country that are open to horse travel.

Horses are forbidden within Peter Lougheed Provincial Park, with one exception. The trail to Elbow Lake provides ideal access to the valleys of the Elbow and Sheep rivers. As such, it is used mainly as a staging area for multiple-day excursions.

Throughout the Sibbald, Elbow, Sheep, and Highwood regions, horseback riding is a popular way to traverse the trails and to access remote areas. Most of the day rides are focused around the numerous equestrian campgrounds and trailheads. Places like Etherington Creek in the Highwood area, Dawson in the Sibbald area, Little Elbow along Highway 66, Mesa Butte along the McLean Creek Trail, and Sandy McNabb and Bluerock in the Sheep Valley provide facilities for overnight camping with horses.

When riding in the Elbow Valley, particularly south of Highway 66, be aware that wild horses also roam the area,

Kananaskis has 825 km (513 mi.) of horseback trails

Mountain Bike Trails

- Prairie View
- Stoney
- Jewell Pass
- Baldy Pass
- Skogan Pass
- Terrace
- Evan–Thomas bike path
- Elbow Lake
- Mist Creek
- Cataract Creek/Etherington Creek
- Oyster Excursion
- Pocaterra
- Whiskey Jack
- Kananaskis Fire Lookout
- Elk Pass
- Sawmill Trail System
- Burstall Lakes
- Cox Hill
- Jumpingpound Ridge
- Tom Snow
- Prairie Creek
- Powderface Creek
- Elbow Loop
- Forget-me-not Rounder
- Wildhorse Trail
- Junction Mountain Fire Lookout
- Sheep Trail
- Watridge Lake-Mount Assiniboine
- Goat Creek
- Banff Trail

and mares have been stolen by wild studs. Avoid bringing mares in heat to this area.

While riding, make sure you bring basic farrier tools, a plastic removable hoof boot, tack repair kit, horse bell, fly wipe, horse brushes, and equine first aid kit. At night, hobble horses that tend to wander, as they can cover quite some distance overnight. Bring your own feed when possible, and take advantage of tie posts, when available, rather than trees. Use a portable bucket and look for rocky areas to water your horses. This will help reduce erosion around streambanks.

There are a few equestrian group campgrounds available by reservation only. They can be booked by calling the Canmore office of Kananaskis Country at (403) 678-5508.

Off-Highway Vehicles

Prefer to have several hundred horses underneath you, rather than just one? In that case, the McLean Creek off-highway vehicle zone may the place for you. With approximately 200 sq. km (77 sq. mi.), and several hundred kilometres of formal and informal trails, the McLean Creek area provides options for every type of equipment and all of your moods. There are staging areas at the McLean Creek Campground, at the north end of the zone, and a second one at Fisher Creek on the south boundary.

Large four-wheel-drive units will do better on the major trails, and these tend to traverse the area from corner to corner. Options include the El-

47

bow River, Silvester, Fisher, Fish Creek, Priddis Creek, McLean, Quirk, and Quirk Ridge trails. Most of these routes are passable, though deep mud holes are often a part of the experience. These trails may also include river fords, but they are generally passable in a 4x4. Remember, the condition varies dramatically, so be prepared for anything.

For dirt bikes, fat-tire trikes, and quad-runners, there are numerous trails that are narrower and more challenging and provide an opportunity to leave the gas guzzlers behind. The steep faces of Mount Barwell are the sole domain of these more agile vehicles. Although helmets are not legally required, they are an essential part of any rider's safety kit. Helmets, sturdy gloves, a kidney belt, good boots, and water- and mud-resistant clothing are recommended.

Within the McLean Creek zone, vehicles are allowed on all cutlines and trails. Trail users are asked to stay on main routes whenever possible, to minimize damage to surrounding areas. Between the signed trails and unsigned cutlines there is an almost endless potential for exploration. Before heading off on a trail, make sure you have a map, in addition to first aid, emergency, and repair kits. A minimum repair kit should include a screwdriver set, duct tape, a wrench set, spark plugs and wrench, a tire repair kit, vice grips, and a spare chain or belt.

McLean Creek off-highway zone

Legal Requirements

When planning a trip to the McLean Creek area, please be aware that rangers regularly patrol the area and regulations are enforced. Off-highway vehicles are governed by the Alberta Off-Highway Vehicle (OHV) Act.

- All vehicles must be licensed as an off-highway vehicle, and must have proper insurance and registration.
- All vehicles must have a stock muffler, exhaust pipes, a spark arrestor, a headlight, and a tail-light.
- Moto-cross bikes are only allowed if they comply with the OHV Act.
- Any vehicle used on public roadways must have a highway license plate, insurance and registration, a

The Elbow-Sheep Wildland Provincial Park

THE ELBOW-SHEEP Wildland Provincial Park was officially announced on January 19, 1996 as part of the Alberta Special Places Program. Since March of 1985, 29 sites have been added to the Alberta Special Places designation.

The park will encompass the headwaters of the Elbow and Sheep rivers, providing protection for approximately 769 sq. km of critical wildlife habitat. It is a popular region for equestrian, hiking and mountain bike travel, not to mention fall hunting and winter snowmobile traffic. It remains to be seen how the change to park status will affect the future of activities like snowmobiling and hunting in the area. The announcement was only the first in a long line of steps required to establish the final boundaries and regulations.

The park borders Peter Lougheed Provincial Park on the west, and crosses Highway 40 at the south boundary of that park. In area, the new park is more than twice the size of Peter Lougheed Park's 305 sq. km (122 sq. mi.), making it the largest provincial park in the province.

Rat's Nest cave on Grotto Mountain

horn, signal lights, mirrors, a speedometer, and brake lights.

Snowmobiling

Winter is an amazing time in Kananaskis. Families pack into their cars, head to the mountains, and take advantage of a plentiful supply of snow. Cross-country skiing and downhill skiing seem to be the primary activities, but hot on their tails is snowmobiling. Snowmobiling is ideally suited to the mountains. It's a great family pastime and provides the opportunity to see the mountains while they're covered in a blanket of fresh snow. It also enables the rider to cover large distances through fairly remote, pristine winter wilderness. This is both a blessing and a danger. When conditions are perfect, riding the Elbow Loop Trail in a snowmobile provides the vision of a winter wonderland. As the machine crests the summit of Elbow Pass, with Tombstone Mountain to the west and Mount Cornwall and Banded Peak to the east, there are few places as wondrous.

There can be a dark side, however, to snowmobiling. The ability of a snowmobile to transport people to remote areas with a minimum of fuss can mean an easy ride to tragedy. Suffering through a break-down, far from the nearest road and without the likelihood of passers-by, can be a lonely experience. See the discussion on snowmobile safety for suggestions on how to ensure your trip is a pleasant one.

There are three main areas open to winter snow vehicles. The McLean Creek area, with its diverse trail system, is the best known. Unfortunately, it often suffers from a lack of snow. Also subject to poor snow is the Sibbald Flat snow vehicle zone. Located adjacent to the Sibbald Creek Trail (Highway 68) at the north end of Powderface Trail, it provides a limited snowmobile area, even in good snow. Its real advantage is its access to the Powderface Trail. This summer road is open to snow vehicles in winter, and can be used to access the Elbow Loop Trail. This loop can also be

reached from the McLean Creek area.

In the Highwood area, the Cataract Creek snowmobile area provides an additional 100 km (62 mi.) of trails. This network tends to see more predictable snow and, consequently, plenty of snowmobile traffic. The trails in this network are well marked, although some of the signs are confusing. One of the routes allows access all the way into British Columbia over the Fording River Pass. This route passes over a major avalanche slope, so be extremely cautious in this area.

Snowmobile Safety

It's easy to understand the attraction of snowmobiling, but travelling through remote country during winter weather also brings a touch of danger into the activity. Winter weather can change in a heartbeat, and sudden storms can catch you unaware. Luckily, snowmobiling means heavy snowsuits and sturdy, warm boots. This can be a lifesaver when a break-down occurs or a blizzard blows over the ridge. Here are some additional suggestions to help make your trip pleasant.

- Never head into the backcountry without a good map.
- Always bring a repair kit, which includes a screwdriver set, duct tape, a wrench set, spark plugs and wrench, vice grips, and a spare belt.
- To ease walking out in a serious mechanical breakdown, bring a pair of snowshoes, some extra food, and a warm drink. Don't forget to pack some

matches, a blanket, a tarp, and a flashlight when heading into remote country. You could end up spending the night.

- Learn about avalanche danger. Snow slides are a constant reality in remote mountain valleys. Always check with Kananaskis Country for current avalanche forecasts.

- Watch for the signs of hypothermia. It is characterized by uncontrollable shivering, loss of coordination, slurred speech, and, in severe cases, a desire to sleep. The symptoms come on slowly and can be easily missed.

- In minor cases of frostbite try to warm the area as soon as possible. This will minimize tissue damage. Don't rub the area, and be cautious of burning the injured part by placing it too close to a fire, as the heat may not be felt. If the freezing is severe, do not attempt to thaw the injured part. It will require medical attention and should wait until it can be thawed safely.

Boating

The Kananaskis and Spray valleys have been modified over the years to provide water storage and hydroelectric power. In the process, the levels of the Upper and Lower Kananaskis Lakes, as well as the Spray Lakes, have been raised significantly. During the same period of development, Barrier Lake was created by flooding the Kananaskis Valley behind Barrier Dam. When these programs were imple-

Whitewater canoeist on the Kananaskis River

mented, they were very controversial. George Pocaterra, an early prospector and trapper in the area, felt hydro development had completely destroyed the character of the valley. Today, people travel from all over the world and marvel at these giant mirrors of the surrounding peaks.

Boats are becoming increasingly common. Families load up the boat, the tent, and the kids and head to the mountains for the weekend. There are not many large lakes on the eastern slopes that allow boats. Kananaskis Country provides a welcome spot to launch boats and ply the waters of numerous mountain lakes.

Since the lakes were artificially raised, the levels tend to fluctuate dramatically. Beneath the waters, the stumps of ancient forests still defiantly hold their ground. As levels drop, the danger of hitting these roots with your boat's propeller increases. For most large boats it's a hard paddle if things go wrong, so prepare for contingencies. Keep your

speeds low and watch for signs. In posted areas the speed is limited to 12 km/hr (7 mi./hr). You won't water-ski at those speeds, but not many people have wanted to ski in these frigid waters.

Canoeing and Kayaking

When the fur traders first made their way westward they used the water. Paddling huge freighter canoes they moved inland. Across most of the plains it was easier to travel

Mirage River Adventures on Kananaskis River

overland than by boat. Once you reached the mountains, forget it! This was the land of the pack train. Once into British Columbia, the horses were traded in for boats, and the traders followed the Columbia River to its source on the Pacific. Today, the mountains see an increasing number of whitewater paddlers testing their skills along many of the local rivers.

In the 1950s, canoeists began to test the waters and found many of the rivers passable. As time passed and tech-

River Guide

FOLLOWING ARE SHORT descriptions of a few of the main river routes in the Kananaskis area. It is not meant to be complete or to be followed as a guide. It is merely designed to highlight some of the principle areas. There are more detailed sources on whitewater paddling available, which will provide the information necessary to safely paddle these rivers.

Kananaskis River

This is the most popular stretch of water in Kananaskis Country. The main route begins at Widowmaker Day Use, 7.9 km (4.7 mi.) south on Highway 40. The put-in is at the bottom of a short trail, in a large natural eddy in the river. Beneath the put-in, a competition-level, Class 3 course has been built. It runs toward Canoe Meadows, where most take out, though you can continue to Seebe Dam along mostly Class 1 and 2 waters. Because it is dam-controlled, you'll need to check with Barrier Information Centre at (403) 673-3985 for current release times.

Highwood River

The Highwood is one of the best paddling rivers in the area, but, like most, the water level drops quickly during the season, making this a spring paddle. The top section, putting in at Highwood Group Camp, provides 10 km (6 mi.) of Class 2 and 3 rapids, with a bit of Class 4 near the lower end. Further downstream, a portage to the right takes you around a Class 5 section.

The next 10 km (6 mi.), from Green Ford Campsite, contains a seemingly endless supply of Class 3 and 4 rapids. There are one or two portages near the end of this stretch. The final 11 km (6.6 mi.), to the Highway 22 junction, provides good intermediate-level paddling with Class 2 being the norm along this pleasant stretch. Take out at the Longview Bridge.

Elbow River

The Elbow can be paddled in numerous sections. The upper stretch from Beaver Flat Campground to Elbow Falls averages Class 1, but don't miss the take-out or you'll end up heading over the lip of Elbow Falls. Lower down, from the put-in at Canyon Creek, the river has numerous rapids of the Class 2 variety along with a Class 3 ledge. The ride is enjoyable and the take-out is at Paddy's Flat Campground.

Sheep River

In high water, this is a great, expert run. With several deep gorges, this river is not for novice paddlers. From Bluerock Campground there are several portages, with the grade averaging Class 2 mixed with lots of Class 4. It is for expert paddlers only, due to sheer canyon walls and limited access to shore. Make sure you read a more detailed description of this route before attempting it.

The lower stretch, below Gorge Creek, is a little tamer. It still has a canyon to be negotiated, but it's less difficult, with Class 2 and a little Class 3 water. The take-out is at Sandy McNabb Campground..

nology improved, kayaks became more prevalent. Well-designed for raging water, they have allowed paddlers to push the limits, and they are now a more common sight in many of the larger rivers.

The rivers along the eastern slopes are often shallow. Boats tend to bounce their way down many watercourses, and fiberglass crafts are rarely up to the task. Modern plastics technology has spawned virtually indestructible materials, and these have become the mainstay for whitewater kayaks and canoes.

Any experienced paddler is quick to admit the power of water. It moves fast and has a force far beyond that of a paddler. This power deserves respect. Learn proper techniques on flat water before attempting swift currents. Always wear a helmet and life jacket, and bring a throw bag for emergencies. A seemingly gentle stream can quickly turn deadly when a log jam appears. Sweepers, which are trees or branches overhanging the stream, are a serious hazard on many local rivers. Stay vigilant, and never paddle alone.

Rafting

Whitewater rafting is becoming more popular every year. As tourism continues to grow, so does our hunger for adventure. Rafting provides an excellent combination of thrill, balanced by the security of professionally trained and certified guides. The Kananaskis

Mountain Rescue

SAFETY IS ALWAYS a big concern in the mountains. Time and again, seemingly harmless jaunts end up in a rescue situation. With more and more people venturing into the wilderness, the inevitable result is an increase in the number of potential accidents. George Field is one of Kananaskis Country's rescue specialists. When someone gets injured, it's his job to make sure that systems are in place to ensure a quick and appropriate response. "What's really important in my area is the training, that we have a staff and we know what their standards are, so that we can put them into rescue situations that they are comfortable in." The training is diverse. It includes training in wilderness first aid, mountain climbing, organized rope and cable rescue, ski mountaineering, avalanche and snow study, search management, and moving-water rescue.

Kananaskis Country has taken over the search and rescue component of the Royal Canadian Mounted Police (RCMP) mandate. Field has been part of the Rescue Program since 1982, and a certified mountain guide since 1985. In the summer of 1986, three planes went down in eight days in Kananaskis. On June 6, a small plane carrying biologist Orval Pall and his pilot disappeared. A second plane, searching for Pall, crashed into the side of Mount Lougheed. On June 14, a military twin otter, also engaged in the search for Pall, crashed and burned, killing all eight on board. Eleven people had died looking for two. As luck would have it, Pall's plane had also been destroyed, killing both him and his pilot. The carnage included 13, but would reach 22 by the end of summer. That was one of the worst years in the short history of Kananaskis.

Although the rescues vary dramatically, no one group seems to stand out when it comes to incidents of rescue. However, scrambling—climbing without ropes—has become increasingly popular, and this has led to an increased number of rescues. It's not only climbers being rescued. In fact a very small number of climber rescues take place. Despite more than a thousand climbers on Mount Yamnuska this summer, there was only one rescue on that sheer face. An average would be two or three per year. Sport climbers, like those commonly seen along Highway 40, tend to self rescue. They get back to the highway and do their own evacuations, so exact statistics are difficult to compile.

Kananaskis Country has a voluntary backcountry registration system. This ensures that park staff know your planned route, and when you will be back. You do need to check back upon return. Unfortunately, a very small number of people use the voluntary system. In 1994, there were over 500 documented occurrences (anything officially dealt with) in Kananaskis, but only about 10% involved rescues. Though media attention usually focuses on those involving mountaineers, according to Field the costs of all the minor rescues combined far outweigh those of the large rescues.

Mountain climbers

River is a great place for the rafting initiate. It isn't a float like the Bow River, yet it's not a heart-stopper like the Kicking Horse. With Class 1 to 3 rapids, it has enough white water to ensure some excitement and the added benefit of the great scenery that has made Kananaskis Country so famous.

Fishing

Fishing is an excellent way to relax at some of the area's backcountry lakes or more easily accessible holes. The options are wide open, as long as you pack your fishing license, and your patience.

According to the Alberta Guide to Sport Fishing, Kananaskis Country lies within Fish Management Area 3. Here are some important points to remember when fishing in Kananaskis.

- The general sport-fishing season runs the entire year, except where specifically stated.
- Everyone aged 16–64 needs to have a valid fishing license.
- The limit for bull trout was reduced to zero in 1995 in order to help in the reintroduction of this declining species.
- The general limit for other trout is a total of five trout or Arctic grayling, of which only one may be golden trout, only three may be lake trout, and none may be Arctic grayling smaller than 30 cm (12 in.) in length.

The following lakes in Kananaskis Country have a trout limit of two:

- Aster Lake
- Burns Lake
- Burstall Lakes
- Carnarvon Lake
- Chester Lake
- Commonwealth Lake
- Fortress Lake
- Galatea Lakes
- Headwall Lakes
- Lake of the Horns
- Lake Rae
- Lillian Lake
- Loomis Lake
- Maude Lake
- Memorial Lakes
- Mud Lake
- Picklejar Lakes
- Rawson Lake
- Ribbon Lake
- Rummel Lake
- Three Isle Lake
- Tombstone Lakes
- Watridge Lake

The general limit for mountain whitefish is 10.

- Live fish and live fish eggs cannot be placed in any water except those from which they were taken, and live fish cannot be used as bait.
- All rainbow trout smaller than 25 cm (10 in.) in length taken from flowing water must be released.
- All golden trout smaller

than 35 cm (14 in.) in length must be released.
- Bait bans are in effect on the Bow River.

The Upper and Lower lakes provide excellent big-water fishing. Spray Lake fills many a frying pan with lake trout—summer and winter. Some of the backcountry lakes can quickly make the walk worthwhile, and the main rivers have many quiet eddies where the fish bite.

Mountain Climbing

Rock climbing is very popular. Each year more than a thousand climbers ascend the steep face of Mount Yam-nuska, and, with the increased popularity of the Kananaskis region, the number of climbers is expected to increase.

Sport climbing involves shorter routes, with fixed anchors. An experienced climber leads or climbs the route first. He then can safely belay for the climbers below. Belaying involves progressively taking up the slack in the rope as climbers ascend. That way, if they fall, they only drop a short distance. The lead climbers run the risk of longer falls, as they must be belayed from the base of the cliff. If they place a small wedge to hold their rope into a crack, and then climb 3 m, they risk falling a total of 6 m before the slack is taken up by the chock. Since most of the sport-climbing routes—places like Barrier Bluffs, Wasootch Tower, and Grotto Canyon—are near main roadways, they are popular for quick afternoon forays.

Mountains like Yamnuska involve multiple pitches and thus high potential dangers. There is a seemingly endless number of routes to the summit, including a hiking trail up the rear of the mountain. There are options for novices and experts. Since this is a major climb, it tends to see the largest number of documented accidents. Beware of

Stocked Lakes within Kananaskis Country

NUMEROUS LAKES in the Kananaskis area are stocked annually, most with cutthroat or rainbow trout. Here is a listing of the lakes stocked in 1994. According to representatives of Alberta Fish and Wildlife, this list varies annually. Be sure to check the most recent copy of the Sport Fishing Guide for more current stocking estimates.

Name of Lake	Month Stocked	Amount	Type of Fish	Length (cm)
Allen Bill Pond	August	2,900	Rainbow Trout	25.6
Buller Pond	May	1,300	Rainbow Trout	17.7
Etherington Creek	August	3,300	Cutthroat Trout	4.5
Ford Creek	August	1,200	Cutthroat Trout	4.5
Forget-me-not Pond	August	800	Rainbow Trout	25.6
Fortress Lake	August	600	Cutthroat Trout	4.5
Kananaskis Village Pond	May	200	Rainbow Trout	32.5
Lake Rae	August	2,100	Cutthroat Trout	4.5
Lake of the Horns	August	1,200	Cutthroat Trout	4.5
Lillian Lake	August	1,200	Cutthroat Trout	4.5
Lower Galatea Lake	August	1,200	Cutthroat Trout	4.5
Lower Kananaskis Lake	August	84,300	Cutthroat Trout	4.5
Maude Lake	August	2,300	Cutthroat Trout	4.5
McLean Pond	June, August	3,100	Rainbow Trout	21.5
McLean Pond	May, June	3,890	Rainbow Trout	17.8
Mount Lorette Ponds	August	2,400	Rainbow Trout	25.6
Ribbon Lake	August	1,900	Cutthroat Trout	4.5
Sibbald Creek Beaverponds	September	70	Eastern Brook Trout	28.3
Sibbald Lake	May	1,700	Rainbow Trout	17.7
Sibbald Meadows Pond	May, July	4,000	Rainbow Trout	20.0
Three Isle Lake	August	3,300	Cutthroat Trout	4.5
Upper Galatea Lake	August	1,000	Cutthroat Trout	4.5
Upper Kananaskis Lake	August, September	43,800	Rainbow Trout	24.0

Beginner's luck

many people head out with little or no training, and risk their lives. Climbing requires very specific knowledge. Don't let your friends teach you—take a course.

Hunting

Each autumn, hunters descend on Kananaskis and head into the backcountry in hopes of bagging the big one. Within certain areas, such as provincial parks, hunting is prohibited, and it is important to know these exclusions. The equestrian parking lots become extra busy at these times, as hunters head into the backcountry on multi-day excursions for elk, mule and white-tail deer, sheep, moose, black bear, and even cougar. Black bears are also hunted during April and May. Game birds taken throughout Kananaskis include ruffed, blue, and spruce grouse, ptarmigan, ducks, and geese. The seasons open near the beginning of September, and run through to the end of November. Ducks and geese are hunted until Dec. 23.

The hunting regulations for Alberta run in excess of 80 pages. It's critical that hunters familiarize themselves with the rules relevant to Kananaskis. Hunters may also choose to donate the hides of their animals to the Alberta Fish and Game Association. This non-profit organization uses the money raised from selling the hides to help acquire critical wildlife habitat within the province. It's one more way that hunters are helping to preserve the resources they enjoy. For information call (403) 437-2342.

sudden storms that can catch you unaware and expose you to the dangers of lightning.

Scrambling is becoming more popular. This involves climbing without ropes. Many summits can be ascended without ropes, but require extensive experience and a much higher skill level. This is one area where the Rangers have experienced a rapid increase in rescues, and they highly discourage this form of climbing.

The most important thing to keep in mind is safety. Too

Poaching

SEVERAL YEARS AGO a hunter had his photo, along with his trophy sheep, published in a local newspaper. According to the article, he had taken the sheep more than 100 km (60 mi.) from the Sheep River Valley. To local biologists studying the sheep within the Sheep River Wildlife Sanctuary, something seemed very wrong indeed. They knew that sheep. They had become intimately acquainted with all the sheep in the sanctuary, and, had learned to recognize each from a distance. This helped them keep "tabs" on the various individuals. When they insisted that animal could not have been taken at the location listed in the article, Fish and Wildlife Officers and Park Rangers began to investigate.

During hunting season, Park Rangers routinely keep records of the license plates of vehicles parked at the various recreation areas adjacent to the Sheep Sanctuary and sure enough, when this hunter claimed to be at some distant location, his car was parked within the Sanctuary boundaries. Strike one for the anti-poaching patrol.

The vast majority of hunters are honest sportsmen. Their fees help pay for many of the province's conservation programs. Unfortunately, some hunters prefer to follow their own rules, and poaching is always a concern. If you suspect poaching, immediately call Alberta's toll-free poaching line at 1-800-642-3800. If your phone call results in charges being filed, you may even be eligible to receive a reward.

5. The Kananaskis Trail (Hwy. 40)

Barrier Lake and Mount Lorette

The Kananaskis Trail takes you through the most highly travelled corridor of Kananaskis Country. As the most well known and thoroughly developed area, it acts as a funnel, leading most visitors into this picturesque valley. Unfortunately, it also leaves the impression that there is little more to Kananaskis than this one district. I generally recommend visitors use this valley as an introduction to the vast recreational riches that Kananaskis has to offer, and then follow up with visits to some of the other, less travelled areas.

The valley is easy to find. Simply follow the Trans Canada Highway (Highway 1) west from Calgary for approximately 60 km (36 mi.), until you meet the junction with Highway 40. From the south, you can access this area via Longview along Highway 22, southwest of Calgary.

This area was known to the local Stoney Indians for generations. Archaeological sites dating as far back as 6,000 BC have been located within Kananaskis Country. The Stoneys travelled these valleys searching for big game, and later trapped their isolated lakeshores. The valley's European history began with the travels of James Sinclair. He passed through in 1854, bringing settlers to the newly opened Oregon Territory. A few years later he was followed by Captain John Palliser, who did the first detailed surveys. It was also Palliser that dubbed the valley "Kananaskis," after the legend of an Indian named Kananaskis, who had survived a blow to the head by a battle axe.

More recently, it has seen Depression work camps, prisoners-of-war, and endless numbers of sightseers and recreationists. Since the Olympics and the media coverage of the downhill events at Nakiska at Mount Allan, this valley has seen increased pressure from developers. The trick now will be to slow things down, and create a long-term plan to manage growth and maintain the wilderness character that has made this valley so popular.

Make sure you stop in at

Opposite: Mount Kidd

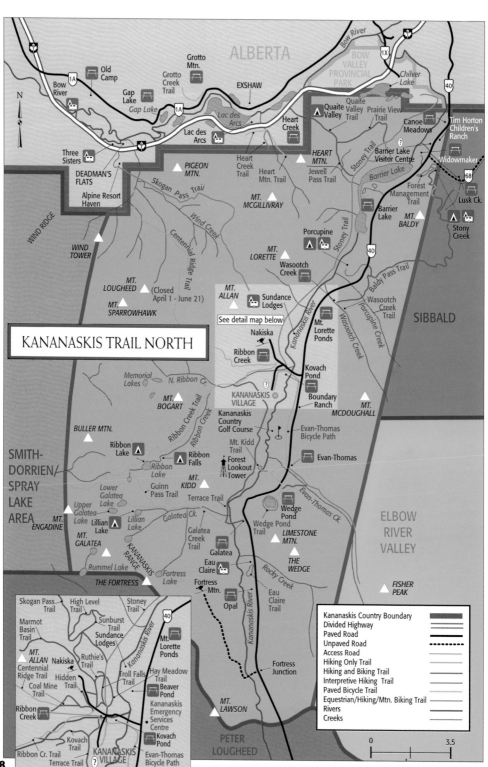

ALBERTA

BOW VALLEY PROVINCIAL PARK

KANANASKIS TRAIL NORTH

SMITH-DORRIEN/SPRAY LAKE AREA

SIBBALD

ELBOW RIVER VALLEY

PETER LOUGHEED

Legend

Kananaskis Country Boundary	
Divided Highway	
Paved Road	
Unpaved Road	
Access Road	
Hiking Only Trail	
Hiking and Biking Trail	
Interpretive Hiking Trail	
Paved Bicycle Trail	
Equestrian/Hiking/Mtn. Biking Trail	
Rivers	
Creeks	

0   3.5

the Barrier Lake Visitor Information Centre on your way south. It provides updated literature and maps, as well as information on current trail conditions and helpful suggestions on how to maximize your time in the area.

Canoe Meadows

The Kananaskis River, like so many of our great rivers, has been dammed in several places, which limits the amount of water flowing downstream. As a peak-flow generator, the water is released at sporadic times, depending on power usage and the requirements of TransAlta Utilities. This leads to a potentially dangerous situation as the river can change from an almost empty channel to a competitive-level whitewater course in a matter of minutes. It is very important to stay out of the channel during low water.

This duality led paddlers to custom design a whitewater course. They used earth movers, added some rocks and other obstacles, and created a Class 3 competition course. Over the past few years it has hosted numerous whitewater events, and sees paddlers challenging its waters even during winter. Canoe Meadows forms the take-out point for paddlers, while the put-in is several kilometres further south, at Widowmaker Day Use. For information on dam release times, contact the Barrier Lake Information Centre at (403) 673-3985.

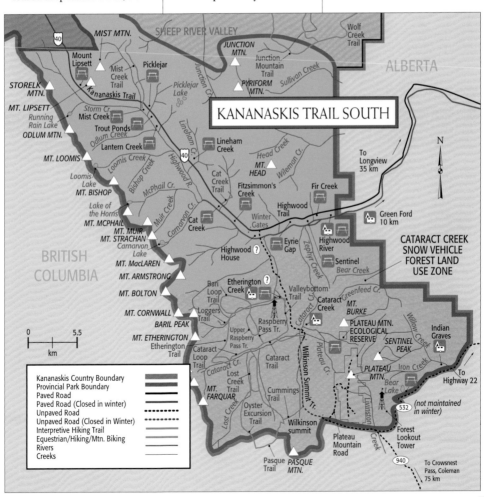

KANANASKIS TRAIL SOUTH

Legend:
- Kananaskis Country Boundary
- Provincial Park Boundary
- Paved Road
- Paved Road (Closed in winter)
- Unpaved Road
- Unpaved Road (Closed in Winter)
- Interpretive Hiking Trail
- Equestrian/Hiking/Mtn. Biking
- Rivers
- Creeks

0 5.5 km

Mount Baldy and Barrier Lake

Tim Horton Children's Ranch

Tim Horton, a Canadian hockey great, had a great love for children. He felt very lucky in life and wanted to help those less fortunate than himself. Shortly after his untimely death in 1974, the Tim Horton Children's Foundation was conceived. Operating four wilderness camps across

Eagle Migration

EAGLES ABOUND in the mountains, especially during spring and fall. Not too long ago it was believed that most of the continent's eagles migrated along routes that kept them out of Kananaskis. Amazingly, several years ago a field biologist from Calgary, Peter Sherrington, discovered a previously unknown migratory route taking large numbers of golden eagles right over the area.

The numbers are quite astounding—approximately 5,500 eagles pass by on each migration, and, according to Sherrington, have likely done so for more than 11,000 years.

During Sherrington's self-financed studies he has noticed that the older eagles seem to appear earliest in the spring, followed by the younger birds. They make use of relatively stable air masses during late February and early March. In the fall, the young birds are the first to vacate the north country and head for warmer climes.

Since eagles mate for life, they usually travel in mated pairs, interacting little with other individuals on the migration. Sherrington describes the migrating birds as being similar to people in rush hour. We may be going to the same place, but our interaction with other commuters is minimal.

When is the best time to watch for eagles? They can be seen beginning at around 9:00 a.m., with the numbers increasing until 4:00 or 6:00 p.m. In autumn, the numbers begin to drop off at around 5:00 p.m. The late-afternoon preference is likely related to the strong thermals created at that time as air rises. This makes travel easier and allows them to fly at speeds of 100–120 km/hr (60–72 mi./hr.).

Bald eagle

The area surrounding Barrier Lake and Mount Lorette is one of the prime spots for watching the migration. In fact Peter Sherrington spends around six months a year in this area for his field studies. To celebrate the migrations, Canmore and Banff alternate with an annual event called the Festival of Eagles.

Mount Lorette and Barrier Lake

Canada, it provides facilities for children who might not otherwise have an opportunity to go to summer camp. The camps help the dreams of many children come true.

The Kanaskis ranch consists of a spacious three-floor lodge and four rustic cabins. There is also a 669-sq.-m (7,200-sq.-ft.) recreation hall, a full western town, a teepee village, and a stable and corral. The corral holds 40 horses during the summer months.

The Foundation is funded by Tim Horton's Donuts store owners and private donations. The store owners work with local schools, churches, and affiliated helping agencies to select children that would benefit from visiting the camps. Each year over 4,000 children attend 10-day camps at the various facilities, and the memory of Tim Horton lives on in their smiles.

University of Calgary Environmental Research Centre

This site holds a lot of history. Over the years it has helped usher in many of the changes this valley has seen. Today it is a quiet educational site used for Environmental Research.

Like many developments in Canada and the U.S., this site owes its existence to the Depression of the 1930s. During those difficult times, cities were deluged with unemployed men. There was no work to be had, and provincial and federal governments were forced to take action. The sight of long lines of hungry souls waiting outside soup kitchens and relief stations is forever burned into the memories of many seniors.

In an attempt to deal with the endless numbers of unemployed, the government began a series of relief camps to provide work, along with token amounts of money, for these

men. The wage was a whopping 20 cents a day, and the men descended upon the wilderness of western Canada. Some headed toward the mountains of Banff and Jasper to build the Icefields Parkway. Others headed to the Kananaskis, where the government leased 160 sq. km (64 sq. mi.) of the valley for a research centre. The purpose of the facility was to do research on spruce and lodgepole pine in the area.

The first order of business was the building of a series of 12 x 6-m frame huts covered with tar paper. These housed the workers. Shortly afterward, they built a mess hall, a cook house, a wash house, latrines, and a log cabin for an office. Far from finished, they cleared several fire roads, built picnic shelters, thinned some stands of timber, and cleared some old burn sites. In time, this camp served as headquarters for four relief camps built in the area. Their tenure was short lived. By June of 1936,

61

most of the work had been completed, and the relief program was discontinued. The site didn't remain quiet for long, however. As tensions flared in Europe and war broke out, the camp was taken over for internment of German and Italian nationals whose loyalties were questioned.

While the war in Europe raged, work at the Kananaskis Forest Experimental Station was scaled down significantly. With victory, research began to pick up once again. During the next few years, trees were thinned, soil studies were undertaken, and exotic trees were planted. The period of 1951–60 was unusually busy—Forest and Fish and Wildlife officers trained there as part of the Alberta Forest Service Training School. Forestry research ceased in 1969. However, in 1966 an area was leased to the University of Calgary for the purpose of environmental research.

Barrier Lake

The first mountain lake visible along Highway 40, Barrier Lake takes its name from the imposing mountain along its eastern shore. Mount Baldy was originally known as Barrier Mountain, and formed a natural obstacle to travellers following the Kananaskis River prior to its metamorphosis into a man-made lake.

The area in which the lake sits today was first cleared by German prisoners-of-war during the summer of 1945. Although they could not be required to perform such manual labour according to the Geneva Convention, they enjoyed the work, and were paid

Prisoners of War

Barracks at Kananaskis POW camp

AS THE SITUATION in Europe deteriorated into war, a former work camp beneath the slopes of Mount Baldy was converted and utilized as an internment camp for German nationals. Shortly thereafter, Italians of questionable loyalty were also added to the growing population of internees. The government later released most of the detainees, and those still being held were removed to camps elsewhere. This left the facility vacant, so it was upgraded to hold up to 700 German prisoners of war.

Kananaskis Camp 130—Seebe, as it became known, was inundated with prisoners, primarily commissioned officers with a few enlisted men sent to perform those tasks that were below the dignity of the officers. Over the next several years, the biggest difficulty for the prisoners was finding creative ways to overcome boredom. Some found solace in work—they were paid 50 cents a cord to chop wood and $3.50 a day to work for Calgary Power on hydro pro-

jects within the valley. Others retreated into the arts and actually had shows in local communities, including Canmore. Still others managed to talk the commandant into allowing them to leave the camp to climb local mountains, like Baldy Mountain behind the camp, as long as they promised not to escape, which none attempted while free on these passes.

Also, according to the Geneva Convention they had to be fed food of similar quality and quantity as Canadian troops overseas. Many locals, who were experiencing severe rationing, felt the prisoners were being treated better than the people who lived in the valley. The POWs even managed to supplement their monthly pint of beer with a few hidden stills.

As the war ended, many would look back fondly at their years in Kananaskis, and some even attempted to remain in Canada after the war. Although they were all returned to Germany, many subsequently emigrated.

Mount Kidd and the Kananaskis Inn

Sunset over the Lodge at Kananaskis

$3.50 a day. The timber, not of saleable quality, was burned. Two years later, on July 18, 1947, the Barrier Plant opened with a capacity of 12,900 kW, and a head of 47 m (155 ft.). The reservoir is 308 ha (770 acres) in size and has a storage capacity of 44,530,000 m^3 (1.5 trillion ft.^{3}). Calgary Power, now known as Trans Alta Utilities, uses Barrier as a peak-flow generator. As such, it provides power to the grid during those times of day when the draw is at its maximum.

Although the lake is not natural, few people complain as they drive past its turquoise waters. Its shores are used by picnickers, hikers, mountain bikers, and other curious explorers.

Mount Lorette Ponds

The five ponds of Mount Lorette were formed by diverting the Kananaskis River. Their linear nature provides an ideal place for families to cast a line for some of the regularly stocked rainbow trout. Completely wheelchair accessible, it is also popular with visitors to William Watson Lodge, and was designed to accommodate physically challenged individuals. The fish are not huge, but they can be more than enough to keep kids of all ages happy during family outings.

During busy summer weekends the site is a buzz of activity, as families and special needs users flock to the site. The fish are visible in the shallow waters, so they disappear rapidly after stocking. In August of 1994, the ponds were stocked with 2,400 rainbow trout, averaging 25 cm (10 in.) in length. Generally the stocking program is fairly consistent on an annual basis, but you'll want to check with local Fish and Wildlife offices for current information.

Ribbon Creek

The area around Ribbon Creek is one of the busiest in all of Kananaskis Country. With over 10,000 hikers each year, the Creek is rarely without hikers or skiers exploring its course.

In 1947, the Kananaskis Exploration and Development Company began exploiting coal reserves on Mount Allan. To accommodate the miners and support staff, bunkhouses were built and a village soon sprung up adjacent to the site. Before long, a school, a small store, and a snack bar were added to the growing village. On the opposite side of Ribbon Creek, Calgary Power built its own set of bunkhouses. The growing community was known as "Ribbon Crik" or "the camp," but its official name was "Kovach," named after the district

Mike Mitrovic, Owner of Mirage Adventures

MIKE MITROVIC is one of the pioneer businessmen of Kananaskis Country. Beginning operation in 1986, when there was little market for raft tours on the Kananaskis, he was the first commercial operator on the river. With a retail store in Kananaskis Village, he is able to market his programs to guests at the facility while also providing tours on the Red Deer River.

Mitrovic sees Kananaskis as an area with increasing opportunity, but difficult political balances. With increasing tourism comes the possibility of controls. He has found himself becoming more involved politically to help influence the direction of tourism and government interaction in the Kananaskis area. He has been President of the Professional River Outfitters Association of Alberta since 1989, and has sat on an advisory committee for Kananaskis Country as well as on the Kananaskis River Users Committee. Through these various projects, he has been able to help resolve difficulties in projecting water flow through Barrier Dam, and has also had a say in how licensing and professional tour operations on the river interact with Kananaskis Country's political machinery.

His operation has mush-

Mike Mitrovic

roomed over the past few years to include rafting on both the Kananaskis and Red Deer rivers, as well as hiking, mountain and road biking, cross-country skiing, sightseeing, orienteering competitions, and even event planning. Many of his packages involve two activities, like cycling or horseback riding, and rafting.

Mike has split his company into three different facets: Mirage Adventure Tours, Kananaskis River Adventures, and Mirage Sports Store. Kananaskis River Adventures is devoted to the long-term development of just the Kananaskis River, while Mirage has other components, like the Red Deer River operation. The retail store allows them to earn off-season revenue with product sales.

His business premise is simple—provide guaranteed service and constantly evolving products. To complement this, he provides employment guarantees for his staff. This helps him attract quality people, and keep them. Not many tourism operators can claim this. With 18 full-time guides, Mitrovic has the largest staff of any Kananaskis river operator. He pays his staff well, and can keep them busy on a full-time basis.

"I think Kananaskis Country and Canmore are going to develop very quickly...and that's why we're looking at investing in the future. And I've got to do it now, not five years from now when it's too expensive," says Mitrovic. "In this industry, if you get greedy, you burn your own bridges. If you go shy on service...then you're not going to last long...There's enough business for everybody...I think competition's good for you."

Mirage hosted the Canadian Classic, a national whitewater raft race, which provided the company with marketing exposure it could never have afforded on its own, not to mention repeated coverage on TSN (The Sports Network). The event was televised on several occasions.

Ribbon Lake

ranger, Joe Kovach.

During its peak, 150 men worked for the company. The coal was removed on site and then trucked to a tipple on the Stoney Reserve. Even with a capacity of 75 tons/h., the mine was short lived. Much of the market for coal was making the change to oil and in February of 1952, the mine shut down for good. With the closing of the mine, the buildings were left to the elements. It wasn't long before the Calgary Power employees also moved on. In 1976, the Alberta Government decreed that there would be no more mining permits within Kananaskis Country.

Kananaskis Village

Kananaskis Village officially opened on December 20, 1987, shortly before the Olympics. It was located to attract year-round tourism, and is positioned between the Olympic ski hill—Nakiska at Mount Allan—and the 36-hole Kananaskis Golf Course. It consists of three hotels: the Lodge at Kananaskis, the Kananaskis Inn, and the Hotel Kananaskis.

The largest of the hotels, the Lodge at Kananaskis is operated by Canadian Pacific Hotels, and contains 251 rooms, including 58 suites. It also contains a large conference centre, with facilities for upwards of 800 people. The dining scene provides a wide selection, from Western cuisine at Peaks Dining Room, to Japanese selections at The Samurai. A large fireplace in the lobby, with pleasant seating adjacent to it, provides a nice spot to relax.

The Hotel Kananaskis, also a CP Hotel, provides for a more exclusive resort experience. The 68 rooms are large, and all boast a mountain view. The beds are king size and the rooms grand. This is a five-star property, and provides all the perks and conveniences that go with such a designation.

Across the small pond from the Canadian Pacific properties is the Kananaskis Inn. This Best Western hotel provides reasonable rates and a less pretentious atmosphere. Its 96 rooms provide comfortable accommodation, and the facility is popular with families. Relax in the evening at Woody's Pub. Meeting facilities are also available.

The Village Centre provides numerous services to visitors not staying in the hotels. They have an information desk with current trail information, brochures, and postal services. A large fireplace with ample seating provides a welcome spot to plan the day's activities. Rentals of sports equipment are available, and after a hard bike ride, why not take in their health spa? Complete with sauna, whirlpool, and steam room, it provides a relaxing way to finish off the day.

For the fun-seeker, the village area boasts a children's playground, a toboggan hill, an outdoor firepit, tennis courts, a sports field, horseshoe pitches, an outdoor volleyball court, and a croquet site. Nearby, a helicopter landing pad offers scenic rides or quick access to local communities like Canmore.

Ribbon Creek Hostel

After the town of Kovach was abandoned, the schoolhouse was purchased in 1960, by the Canadian Youth Hostel Association (CYHA). They paid the princely sum of $105 for the old structure. Before long, renovations were required, and in 1963, Jim Lisoway, local president of the hostel association, decided to make the building an A-frame. Unfortunately, the attempt was less than successful. As Ray Marriner, president of the Mountain Region put it:

"We started out by dismantling the roof, then sawing the side walls off about three feet from the ground. We then used the completely inadequate lumber from the old rafters to make the A rafters. A properly constructed A-frame building is one of the strongest structures, but our new hostel was anything but! By the time the shingles were applied to the roof the whole building was so unstable that the sides of the roof would flap in and out in a strong breeze."

Draftsman Neil Worley divided the building into two floors and managed to make it more stable. By 1969, a larger hostel was needed for the in-

Nakiska at Mount Allan

Olympic ski hill

THIS SKI HILL hosted, and was built specifically for, the alpine events of the 1988 Winter Olympics. It consists of 70% intermediate, with 16% novice, and 14% expert runs. The vertical drop totals 760 m (2,494 ft.). Since the hill was designed to move huge numbers of spectators during the games, it has an incredible capacity—8,620 skiers per hour. Lifts include two detachable quad chairs, one triple chair, and one double chair. To ensure an ample snow supply, snow-making facilities reach 85% of the hills surface. Today Nakiska is a popular family ski hill, due largely to the lack of crowds and the hill's proximity to Calgary. It is also much less expensive than its more famous counterparts in Banff.

Not only a winter resort, during late summer it hosts the annual "Mozart on the Mountain" event. This huge event, which in 1995 drew upwards of 13,000 spectators, is a presentation of the Calgary Philharmonic Orchestra, in partnership with the ski hill. The spectators sprawl all over the lower slopes of the ski

hill. After all, could there be any better way to take in some fine classical music while still enjoying a day in the mountains?

Despite this popularity, the site was almost never built. There was a long debate over potential locations for the Olympic downhill events, and this site was not always the front runner. Mount Sparrowhawk, along the Smith–Dorrien/Spray Trail, was also in the running. In November of 1982, the final word came down—Mount Allan was in, Sparrowhawk was out. The Calgary Olympic Development Association had made its final decision, and a new facility would be constructed to the exacting specifications of the International Olympic Committee. Right up until the games ended, the area was under heavy pressure to perform. Skeptics predicted that there would be no snow and the events would flop. In the end, the mountain performed flawlessly. A few wind delays postponed some events, but to the 20,000 fans spread all over the hill, the events were perfect.

Kananaskis golf course

Columbian ground squirrels

creasing number of guests. Before long, fundraising was complete, and on July 20, 1970, the doors to the new hostel opened. Designed by Worley, it was again expanded in 1971, with the addition of a large common room, four family rooms, and separate quarters for the house parents. Today the hostel is one of the most popular in the Southern Alberta Hosteling Association's chain of mountain hos-

tels. Busy year round, it seems to change as Kananaskis Country does.

Boundary Ranch

Originally called Boundary Stables, this ranch has grown substantially since it first opened. Today it houses all manner of groups and individuals, providing a western "cowboy" experience. Trail rides radiate out from the stables, and the ranch's guides

will take you on rides to match your ability.

Recreational rides during the peak summer months, followed by extended wilderness hunting trips during the fall, keep them busy. With facilities for large groups, the Ranch attracts conference-goers looking to kick up their heels, and tour groups seeking to take advantage of the guided horseback rides. Evening functions provide plenty of food, dancing, and the relaxing feeling that comes with hangin' out at the ranch.

In 1989, the ranch was featured in the Don Johnson movie "Dead Bang," as the setting of a neo-nazi camp. The barn was renovated, a small stage and fireplace were added, and the walls were redone with tongue-and-groove cedar. When filming concluded, the renovations were left in place. Suddenly Boundary Ranch had a dance hall,

67

that is, once they built a new barn.

Owner Rick Guinn is no stranger to movies himself. As the star of an earlier western film called "Buffalo Rider," he played a cowboy who rode a buffalo instead of a horse—not a simple feat. His father, Alvin Guinn, originally operated another local guest ranch, the Rafter Six Resort. Also, a nearby pass, Guinn's Pass, is named after Rick Guinn's father.

Kananaskis Country Golf Course

Golf is one of the world's fastest-growing recreational activities, and this course has to be seen to be believed. With 36 challenging holes, the government spent in the neighbourhood of $36 million on its development. Construction began in 1978, and the course officially opened, with 27 of its 36 holes completed, on July 22, 1983. During the development phase, Bob Parkin, the provincial government's project manager, stated : "It will be a public course for Albertans, but it will be a world-class standard." In a good year the course averages over 75,000 rounds of golf during their season, from May to September or October.

Almost 100 m (300 ft.) higher than the Banff Springs golf course, the Kananaskis golf course's elevation allows golfers to hit the ball slightly farther, and use less club, than lower courses. It has numerous par-5 holes, with one topping out at 550 m (600 yd.). An 18-hole round can be as long as 6,000 m (6,560 yd.).

As it's difficult to drop in, you'll need to reserve tee times by calling 261-GOLF in Calgary, 463-GOLF in Edmonton, or (403) 591-7272 from all other locations. Reservations are taken up to 60 days in advance.

Wedge Pond

Wedge Pond began life as a tiny, shallow body of water. With the building of the Kananaskis Golf Course, approximately 300,000 m^3 (10.5 million ft.^{3}) of gravel were removed from it to use as topsoil and contouring material. Today, it has been landscaped and converted into a put-and-take fishing pond. Lying beneath its namesake mountain, it provides a mirror-like reflection of its surrounding peaks, including Mount Kidd to the west and The Fortress to the south.

Occasionally stocked with rainbow trout, the pond is an excellent place for a family outing. It has numerous picnic sites with firepits, and is at the south end of the Evan–Thomas paved bicycle path.

Fortress Mountain Ski Area

Fortress Mountain is one of the premier family ski hills in the mountains. It doesn't offer the variety of terrain found at Sunshine or Lake Louise, but it

Tick Talk

TICKS ARE QUITE prevalent in this area, so check for them before your day's activity is done. Their favourite spots are any warm moist area they can find. These include in the hairline, armpits, and pubic area, and behind tight-fitting clothing (bra and underwear straps).

Similar in appearance to a small spider, ticks have a triangular body and eight legs. To feed, they insert their mouthparts into the skin—only their mouthparts. After anchoring themselves with a secreted glue, they slowly draw blood from you until they've had their fill and drop off. Females swell to several times their body size while males take only a small amount.

Ticks hang on to low-lying vegetation and as you walk by they hitch a ride. Since they usually don't crawl too far, you can discourage them by tucking your pant legs into your socks. If they don't find a suitable site, they simply drop off.

Removal is quite easy. Grab the tick and slowly but steadily pull it out. Make sure that the mouth parts don't break off and remain in the wound. If they do, remove them with a sterilized needle, and then use a little disinfectant on the wound.

While ticks can cause Rocky Mountain Spotted Fever, the incidence is quite low. Lymes Disease, another malady transmitted by ticks, has not been recorded in Kananaskis.

Ticks are one of the very few drawbacks of living in the mountains, but with a little attention they cause very little discomfort. Enjoy your hike and remember to check for hitchhikers.

does offer excellent ski runs with short lift lines, and great snow. After a heavy snowfall, Fortress is a superb choice for fresh powder.

Development of "Snowridge Ski Area," as the site was first named, began in 1966. The development proceeded at the 1,950-m (6,435-ft.) elevation of Fortress Mountain, at the end of a winding 8-km (4.8-mi.) road.

When it opened in 1969, the basic facilities included a single chairlift, two T-bars, and a 140-bed hotel.

Within a year, Brewster Transportation acquired the hill, but was no more successful, and after a year and a half the operation went bust. Following a test during the 1974/75 season, while still in receivership, the hill began operation. During the summer of

1975 a triple chairlift was constructed. Although the hill has changed hands numerous times, it remains an enduring part of the Kananaskis landscape. Today it is operated by Skiing Louise, as is Nakiska farther north on Highway 40. Be forewarned, however—after a large dump of snow, the access road can be a slippery, snowy challenge.

Mount Kidd

Mount Kidd reflected in the Kananaskis River

ONE OF THE most impressive mountains in the Kananaskis Valley, Mount Kidd dominates the scenery as you travel south beyond Kananaskis Village, or north past Galatea Creek. As a classic example of a Main Range mountain, its thick limestone layers tower above the surrounding valley. On its north shoulder, a tiny

fire lookout perches high above Kananaskis Village.

This peak is named after Stuart Kidd (1883–1956), an early Alberta rancher who also managed Scott and Leeson's Trading Post at Morley. Following his stint at Morley, he operated the Brazeau Trading Company in Nordegg. The mountain was

named in 1907 by D.B. Dowling, the surveyor responsible for assessing the value of the Ribbon Creek coal seams in 1903.

Kidd was fluent in the Stoney language and eventually became an honorary chief in 1927. He was given the Stoney name "Tah-Osa" which translates to "Moose Killer."

Wedge Pond

O'Shaughnessy Falls

WATERFALLS ARE always a welcome site along roadsides, even if they are not completely natural. This falls was built by John O'Shaughnessy in 1973, during upgrading of Highway 40. When he tried to divert the water from this small stream through a culvert, it stubbornly refused to cooperate and continued to spill over the highway. By building this small falls, the problem was solved. He followed up with a wishing well and some general landscaping.

Unfortunately vandals damaged the falls in 1981, and for several years it looked like it would continue to deteriorate. Thankfully, Exshaw resident Warren Harbeck circulated a petition asking that the government

O'Shaughnessy Falls

repair the site. After 400 people signed their names, the government announced that it would fund restoration. The announce-

ment was made in September of 1983, and the repairs done shortly after. It is now a pleasant place to stop and watch the water tumble over numerous steps on its way towards the Kananaskis River. The name O'Shaughnessy Falls was officially approved on December 5, 1984.

Occasionally people bring water jugs to fill. However, this is not recommended since this water, like most local streams, must be suspected of containing *Giardia lamblia*. This small organism can cause a variety of unpleasant symptoms collectively known as "beaver fever." Better to let the water flow, and drink from a proper tap.

The Battle of Jutland and the Canadian Rockies

ONE OF THE most pivotal battles of World War I occurred off the Danish coast of Jutland. The only major naval engagement of the war, it dragged out over two days—May 31 and June 1, 1916. The battle began between the battle cruiser squadrons of Germany's Franz von Hipper and British Admiral David Beatty. The H.M.S. Galatea, flagship of Britain's 1st Light Cruiser Squadron, fired the opening volley. Eventually, the battle escalated to include both main fleets—the British, commanded by Admiral Sir John Jellicoe, and the German, under Admiral Rienhard Scheer.

British losses were immense, but the Germans were prevented from breaking the Allied blockade. For the remainder of the war, the German high fleet never left port again. The Allies lost many more sailors, but the battle is seen as a draw. In terms of the war, it was a turning point.

Throughout the Rockies, a seemingly endless number of peaks commemorate this battle. Mounts Inflexible and Nestor honour battleships of the same name. While Mount Nestor remains, its namesake was sunk during the battle. Mounts Chester, Cornwall, Engadine, Galatea, and Glasgow were

named for many of the battle cruisers in the engagement. The battle cruiser Indefatigable (Mount Indefatigable) exploded after being hit by five shells fired from the German battleship Vonder Tann. Only two of its 957-member crew survived. The Invincible (Mount Invincible), part of the 3rd Battle Cruiser Squadron, was sunk, and only six of its 1,034-member crew survived. The cruiser H.M.S. Warspite (Mount Warspite), on the other hand, was nicknamed "The Old Lady," and survived both world wars.

Kananaskis Lakes from Opal Range

Kananaskis Lakes Trail

This section of Kananaskis Country is one of the most popular—and most developed—recreation areas. The facilities along the Kananaskis Trail are treated at length in the next chapter, *Peter Lougheed Provincial Park*.

Just south of the junction with the Kananaskis Lakes Trail, a winter gate limits access south on Highway 40. The highway passes through critical winter wildlife habitat, and is closed between December 1 and June 15 to reduce impact during this sensitive season. In winter, cross-country skiers traverse this road, and in spring, before it opens to vehi-cle traffic, it is an excellent road to cycle. The road closure extends all the way to the Highwood Junction, where Highways 940 and 541 meet.

Valley View Trail

This short side trip, which is located 5 km (3 mi.) south of the Kananaskis Lakes Trail turn-off, provides a winding

Highwood Meadows

DURING THE SHORT alpine summer Highwood Pass comes alive with all manner of wildflowers. Situated at the margin of the treeline, it supports a diversity of alpine plants. In the deep forest cover across the road, many of these plants could not survive. Alpine meadows provide a self-contained ecosystem where these sun-loving plants can endure. Life isn't easy in the alpine. The growing season may only be a few months long and the climate is similar to that of the arctic tundra.

With the melting of winter's heavy snow blanket comes the explosion of flowers into flaming reds and yellows. The paintbrush's deep purple looks as if it has been freshly dipped into a paint can. The western anemone quickly trades in its white flowers for its shaggy seed head, earning the pet name "Hippie Flower." The alpine forget-me-not, with its delicate blue flower, forms groups just large enough to make sure not only that you don't miss them, but that you pull out your camera to record them.

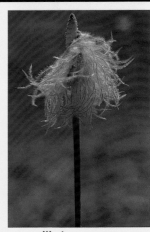

Western anemone

73

alternative to the main highway. Although it meanders only a few kilometres, there are two main viewpoints—Elpoca and Lakeview. From these partially treed pull-outs, you get a panoramic view of the valley and the Upper and Lower Kananaskis lakes. This perspective is only obtained from this route; the main highway doesn't provide this lofty lookout. If you feel energetic, you can scramble higher up the Opal Range and get an unobstructed view of the lakes. This is, however, not a trail, and caution is advised whenever heading off the beaten path.

Rock Glacier

At the base of Mount Rae and the Misty Range, there is a huge debris slope. Although it may seem like a lifeless rock pile, it's a place where nature has left behind a world of opportunity amidst rocky rubble. Not a true glacier, it is a large accumulation of rock that, due to the extreme angle at which it lies, slowly moves downhill, mimicking the movement of its icy namesake.

Within this rocky slope, many animals have taken up residence. The Columbian ground squirrel may utter its peeping call, the tiny pika may call its name, or the golden-mantled ground squirrel may scurry past your feet. Always alert for intrusions of weasels—the only predator able to follow these animals into their rocky home—they keep a constant vigil. Other dangers include hawks, which silently swoop down and carry off unsuspecting residents of the rock pile.

Highwood Pass summit

Highwood Pass

From the junction with the Kananaskis Lakes Trail, the road climbs steadily from 1,700 m (5,610 ft.) until it crests Highwood Pass at an elevation of 2,206 m (7,280 ft.). With the gentle appearance of the pass, it surprises most people to learn that this is the

Chickadees and Nuthatches

IT'S FUNNY HOW we always tend to focus on superlatives—the biggest, the strongest, and the most dramatic. Two of the most common, but rarely noticed, birds in Kananaskis are the black-capped chickadee, and the red-breasted nuthatch.

The chickadee is about 11 cm (4.4 in.) long and has a tiny beak. It has a distinct black cap and throat patch separated by whitish cheeks. Its back is a drab greyish-brown and the underside is lightly coloured. It quickly gives away its presence as it opens its beak and calls out its name: "chick-a-dee-dee-dee." This, along with its distinctive markings quickly identifies this common resident. There are three different types of chickadees living in this area, but the black-capped is by far the most common.

Chickadees eat small insects, larvae, and seeds. Very agile flyers, they can be seen perched upside down as they peck away with their little beaks in search of food. When they take a large seed, they hold it between their feet, and peck away at it until they get at the fleshy meat beneath the shell.

Their neighbour, the red-breasted nuthatch, is equally easy to identify. It has a bluish-gray back, a rusty breast, and a dark head patch and eye streak. Usually you'll see it working its way down a tree, checking behind the tops of the bark scales for anything worth eating. Like the chickadee, it likes insects and seeds, and quickly finds any new bird feeder within its turf.

Like the chickadee, the call of the red-breasted nuthatch is quite distinctive. It's a nasal-sounding "eenk" which can't be confused with any other local bird. You may need someone to point the call out to you for the first time.

Barrier Lake and Mount Baldy from Prairie View Trail

highest engineered road in Canada.

Lying beneath the summits of Mounts Rae and Arathusa of the Misty Range to the east, and the folded slopes of Mount Tyrwhitt of the Elk Range to the west, the location is one of alpine splendour. In all directions the action of glaciers can be seen etched into the rock faces.

From the parking lot, a short, self-guided interpretive trail takes you on a stroll through an exceptional alpine meadow. This is one of the most accessible alpine meadows in the Rockies, and every July the field explodes with flowers such as western anemone.

In the spring of 1994, an interesting encounter took place high up on the pass. A small plane was tracking a local grizzly bear as part of a research study. Suddenly the plane began to experience mechanical problems. An emergency landing was necessary, and the plane managed a rough touchdown on the closed highway along Highwood Pass. As it was the first week of June, the pass had not yet opened for vehicle traffic. Once on the ground, the bear must have figured that turn-about was fair play, and it began to track the wardens, until they found themselves treed by the very bear they had been tracking.

Highwood Junction

As you descend from Highwood Pass and continue the final 35 km (21 mi.) to Highwood Junction, you drop more than 600 m (1,980 ft.) . The narrow valley of the Pass widens dramatically as you approach the Junction. Gradually the prominent faces of the Elk Range give way to the towering cliffs of the High Rock Range. North of the junction the narrow Highwood Range terminates with Mount Head, at 2,782 m (9,181 ft.). Named by Captain John Palliser when he travelled through the valley in 1858, it commemorates Sir Edmund Walker Head (1805–1868), who was Governor-in-Chief of Canada from 1854 to 1861. He was a major contributor to the early work on the concept of confederation, and returned to England in 1861 to became Governor of the Hudson's Bay Company.

This intersection forms an important juncture. It marks the southern extent of the winter highway closure, and provides the option of continuing east to the town of Longview, or heading south on the good gravel of the Forestry Trunk Road. The southern boundary of Kananaskis Country is 24 km (14.4 mi.) south along this road. Once there, you can exit along steep, secondary Highway 532, or continue to the Crowsnest Pass.

East of Highwood Junction the paved highway becomes Highway 541, and meanders through pleasant foothills until it meets the town of

Longview, 35 km (21 mi.) distant. As you travel this stretch, the mountains quickly lose their imposing nature and the foothills become the dominant landform. Passing the eastern boundary, you enter ranching country with its high, grassy, south-facing slopes. Keep your eyes open for golden eagles soaring over-head, on the lookout for ground squirrels.

Forestry Trunk Road

Following the Forestry Trunk Road provides quiet, dusty diversion. Away from the hustle and bustle of Highway 40, you can explore areas of Kananaskis that see very little traffic. The road has a good gravel surface, but during the winter it closes between Cataract Creek Campground and Wilkinson Summit. From the Cataract and Etherington campgrounds a diverse system of summer trails and winter snowmobile trails radiate. Heading west towards the Continental Divide, they pro-

Lost Lemon Mine

THE STORY OF the Lost Lemon Mine is one of the enduring legends of the Canadian Rockies. Like most stories, this tale has grown and changed over the years. The basic tale tells of a group of prospectors who, in 1870, left Tobacco Plains, Montana in search of gold. They planned to prospect along the North Saskatchewan River, a river which still bears some gold today. Along the way, two prospectors, Blackjack and Lemon, headed out on their own.

Senator Dan Riley wrote the classic account of the legend for the Alberta Folklore Quarterly in 1946:

"Blackjack and Lemon found likely showings of gold in the river. Following the mountain stream upwards toward the headwaters they discovered rich diggings from grass roots to bedrock. They sank two pits and, while bringing their cayuses in from the picket line, they accidentally discovered the ledge from which the gold came...

In camp that night the two prospectors got into an argument as to whether they should return in the spring or camp right there. After they had bedded down for the night, Lemon stealthily crawled out of his blankets, seized an axe and split the head of his sleeping partner. Overwhelmed with panic when he realized the enormity of his crime, Lemon built a huge fire and, with his gun beneath his arm, strode to and fro like a caged beast till dawn."

The story doesn't end here. Apparently two Stoney Indians had followed the group and witnessed the entire episode. Later, their chief, Moses Bearspaw, made the braves promise to remain ever silent about the incident. He was afraid the white man would invade their hunting grounds and forever alter their traditional way of life.

Since that time, numerous expeditions have searched for the gold. According to the legend, most of these, at least all that came close to finding the gold, met with tragedy. On several occasions, Lemon tried to lead expeditions to the mine, but whenever he approached the area, he got progressively more agitated. In the end, he was never able to rediscover the location of the gold.

Shortly after Blackjack's death, a mountain man named John McDougall was dispatched to bury the unfortunate prospector. This he did, and was later re-engaged to lead a party back to the site. He never arrived. On his way to meet them he had stopped at Fort Kipp, Montana and drank himself to death.

Lafayette French, the man who had funded Blackjack and Lemon, was also determined to find the mine. For many years French searched for the gold, and it appears that he may have finally succeeded. He wrote to a friend, stating that he had found the mine, but was fatally burned when the cabin in which he was staying burned to the ground. He did not live long enough to share the secret of the mine's location. The gold had thwarted its seekers once again.

Since then, the story has not died. Throughout the past 125 years, many people have been looking for the mine. Numerous small gold rushes have begun through quiet rumour, but none have located the mother lode. Will it ever be discovered? Who knows? But one thing is evident—stories like this add much to the folklore of the Canadian wilderness.

Ribbon Falls

vide excellent views of the surrounding peaks of the High Rock Range. For more information on the trails in this area, see the descriptions at the end of this section.

At the south boundary of Kananaskis Country, Highway 532 steeply winds its way eastward towards Highway 22. Climbing over 200 m (660 ft.) in the first few kilometres, it drops off the summit just to the east of flat-topped Hailstone Butte. Over the next two kilometres, it plummets 300 m (990 ft.) along a gear-grinding gradient. Following the route of a gas pipeline, it winds its way to a junction with Highway 22, through pleasant rolling country. Following its drop off the summit, the gradient becomes more bearable and the driving smooth. This route would not be safe in anything but good conditions, as the steep drop could be-

come dangerous when wet or icy.

Hiking Along the Kananaskis Trail (Hwy. 40)

1. Prairie View

This 5-km (3-mi.) out-and-back trail crosses Barrier Dam before climbing 420 m (1,377 ft.) along an old fire-lookout access road. From the summit of this rocky knoll, the views south to Barrier Lake and Mount Baldy are dramatic and unobscured. The emerald green waters of Barrier Lake reveal their glacial origin. If you feel energetic, scramble up to the site of the old fire lookout and get a panoramic view of the Bow valley. The old lookout tower was moved from a prisoner-of-war camp once located on the opposite side of Barrier Lake. When its duties as a tower were fulfilled, it was returned to the site of

the camp.

The walk across the dam is windy and exposed. On the opposite shore, go right at the first junction and climb gently until a second junction at the 1.3-km (0.8-mi.) mark. Go right for a few steps, and the Prairie View Trail will branch to the left. Steady climbing along a high-quality fire road rapidly takes you to the open, exposed viewpoint along the shoulder of this high, rocky knoll.

At this point you have three options. You can either return the same way you came, you can scramble up to the site of the old lookout, or you can descend the far side towards Jewell Pass Trail. The scrambling can be difficult to negotiate with a bike, but a little perseverance is rewarded with a great downhill slalom course on the opposite side, as you descend to Jewell Pass. The route to the old fire lookout climbs to the right of a large white panel. To the north, the imposing slopes of Mount Laurie (Îyâmnathka), locally known as Mount Yamnuska, mark the beginning of the Front Ranges. To the north-west, Lac Des Arcs' resident cement plant billows smoke into the sky.

For cyclists or hikers doing the loop, the Jewell Pass Trail drops to the left of this panel and provides a 14-km (8.4-mi.) loop option with Stoney Trail.

2. Stoney Trail

Following a power line right-of-way, this trail follows the western shore of Barrier Lake and the Kananaskis River all

Logging

WITH THE COMING of the railway, the forests of the Kananaskis and Spray valleys soon came under the axe. Following surveys from 1883–84 by L.B. Stewart, the area was divided into timber limits. First to the draw was James Walker. A former mounted police constable, his mill operated in the Kananaskis Valley between 1883 and 1886. During this period he employed 15–70 men, depending on the season. In 1884, his sawmill processed two million feet of logs. He later managed the famous Cochrane Ranche, and was a long time civic leader and founding father of Calgary. In 1975, during Calgary's centennial celebrations, Walker was voted the citizen of the century for his long affiliation with that city.

Almost simultaneously, Ottawa lawyer Kutusoff MacFee began planning his own logging operation. On a trip to Eau Claire, Wisconsin, a major timber-producing area in the midwestern U.S., he managed to peak the interest of several key people in that area.

Following an exploratory trip down the Kananaskis and Spray valleys, MacFee acquired the rights to 250 sq. km (100 sq. mi.) of timber along the Spray, Bow, and Kananaskis Rivers. With this, the Eau Claire and Bow River Lumber Company was officially

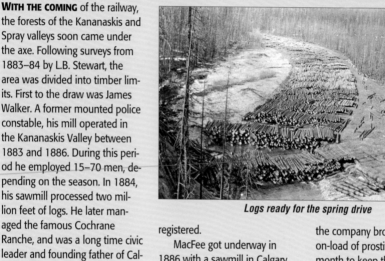

Logs ready for the spring drive

registered.

MacFee got underway in 1886 with a sawmill in Calgary and opened a logging camp along the Kananaskis River, with another near Silver City in Banff National Park. Much of the cutting took place during the winter months, when as much as five million feet of timber was cut. With spring runoff, the logs were floated downstream to the mill in Calgary. The drives were an annual affair, from their inception in 1887 until 1944. Not an overly efficient delivery system, the drives took two months and 30–40 men.

The main camp was located on the site of the present Eau Claire campsite, whereas a secondary camp was located along the south fork of Ribbon Creek. As it was difficult to keep good workers in these isolated camps, the company brought in a wagon-load of prostitutes twice a month to keep the men happy.

By the 1930s and 1940s, the companies were using more and more trucks to move logs to the sawmills. The quality of the wood in the valley dropped following a large fire in 1936. This limited the company to salvage cutting and signaled the beginning of the end of logging in the Kananaskis Valley. The company's mill in Calgary closed in 1945, and the main Eau Claire camp was taken down in 1948 by Joe Kovach, the district ranger at the time. He built a kitchen shelter using some of the scrap lumber. In Calgary, Prince's Island Park was named after Peter Prince, a manager of the Eau Claire Lumber Company between 1886 and 1916.

Mount Galatea from Guinn's Pass

the way to the Ribbon Creek trail system. At 16.5 km (9.9 mi.) one way, it provides an excellent mountain bike trail, but a rather mediocre hiking route. The trail is wide and rolling, with a good grade all the way.

It begins at Barrier Dam day use area. Cross the dam and watch for a sign on the opposite side of the lake. The trail follows the shores of Barrier Lake and then hugs the eastern shore of Mount Lorette as it trends south. As you pass the mid-way point, the views to the southwest open up and the Olympic downhill site—Nakiska at Mount Allan—along with the Wasootch valley to the east, become visible.

As the trail approaches the southern end, it joins with the access road to Nakiska and Kananaskis Village. You can either return the way you came, or turn left and follow High-way 40 north to Barrier Dam day use.

3. Ribbon Creek

The tranquil waters of Ribbon Creek have enticed countless hikers over the years. This is a very busy hiking area, so mountain bikes are forbidden. The trail follows the stream up a narrow valley between Mounts Kidd and Bogart. Mount Bogart got its name from Dr. Donald Bogart Dowling. He was a geologist who examined the coal seams along Ribbon Creek in 1909 and spurred increased interest in mining. The coal seams are still there, but the mining has long since ended.

Summer hiking up the creek provides a pleasant walk amidst the towering peaks and steep mountain walls. Keep your eyes open for a small bird bobbing up and down on the rocks. The dipper, with its well-earned name, has the magical ability to fly underwater to collect insects from between the rocks. Its drab grey colour tends to make it almost invisible, but it is well worth the difficulty to spot.

As you near the 11-km (6.6-mi.) mark, the trail suddenly reaches a rocky barrier at the Ribbon Falls campground. The falls form a delicate ribbon, cascading down the steep face to continue on to the Kananaskis River. Your options are to return on the same trail, or ready yourself for adventure. The trail continues above the rock face, but to access it you must climb 5 m (17 ft.) up the rock face. To assist you, several chains permanently bolted to the face provide solid hand holds. It is still tricky, however, and much easier to climb up than down.

If you make the ascent, the trail continues to climb towards Ribbon Lake, at an elevation of just over 2,000 m (6,600 ft.). This lake mirrors the surrounding peaks. Options here are numerous. You can return on the same trail, climb over the rocky summit of Guinn's Pass, or descend the western side over Buller Pass.

4. Guinn's Pass

Continue 1.5 km (0.9 mi.) farther along the Ribbon Lake trail to its junction with Guinn's Pass. This rugged trail climbs through prime bear habitat as it traverses some lush growth along steep avalanche slopes. As you climb, it becomes exposed and rocky, until near the summit, where it is loose scree. A rocky cairn marks the summit of the pass. A white cross may poke from the top of the cairn.

Ahead of you lies a steep descent along a loose rock trail, towards the junction with the Galatea Trail. Shortly after crossing a bridge, the trail junction leads you upstream to Lillian Lake and the Upper Galatea Lake.

5. Galatea Creek

This trail takes you into remote country and through some enticing grizzly habitat. At the same time, the landscape is divine and the rewards plentiful. Go prepared, and enjoy an isolated wilderness valley. The trail is 6 km (3.6 mi.) one way, and climbs 426 m (1,400 ft.) to Lillian Lake, and an additional 213 m (700 ft.) in 2.4 km (1.4 mi.) to the Upper Galatea Lake.

The trail begins at the Galatea Parking Lot, 34 km (20.4 mi.) south on Highway 40. From the parking lot, it descends quickly to the Kananaskis River, where a high-quality suspension bridge provides easy access to

Martin Nordegg and Canadian Coal

COAL PLAYED A vital role in the opening of the Bow Valley, but most of the mines were short-lived ventures. Martin Nordegg was a pivotal character in the story of the western Canadian coal industry.

Nordegg arrived from Germany in 1906, and represented a German financing company. His backers were looking to invest in Canada's potentially immense mineral industry. When he discovered a thick coal seam on Mount Allan, he collected a large sample as proof of his find . His backers were very impressed, but wanted a second opinion, and so consulted the world's foremost expert on coal at that time, Professor Pontonie. Upon finding the coals origin, the professor immediately called Nordegg a fraud, for according to Pontonie's book, coal did not exist in rocks of the Rockies age. Despite Nordegg's insistence that there were already more than 2,000 tons/day being mined in places like Canmore and the Crowsnest Pass, the Pro-

fessor would not alter his assessment. It appeared the only way to change Pontonie's mind would be to personally show him the seams. Nordegg convinced the Canadian Mining Institute to bring Pontonie to the Rockies, and apparently, as the Professor rode up to the base of Mount Allan and hacked off a few pieces of coal for himself he responded with: "I must rewrite my book!" His report on the quality of the coal in the area helped establish Canada's reputation as a coal producing nation.

Convinced of the value of the coal deposits in the Rockies, Nordegg was recalled once more to assist his backers in their final decisions. Although the Mount Allan site was the ideal place to develop, there was another site further north, in the Brazeau area. It would have been far more difficult, and costly, to develop, as it was much further from the railroad. The banker charged with the final decision took one look at the details of the two sites, and

stated that his choice was very simple—the most expensive site was the best.

Of course Nordegg protested that the Brazeau site was very poorly located, but the banker insisted that "it is easier, and more profitable for me, to find several millions than a few hundred thousand." In fact he would have been happier had Nordegg found an even less accessible local.

Nordegg returned to Canada sickened by European greed, and never again returned to his homeland. During the first world war, almost everything he had worked so hard to build, was taken from him because he was a German national. He eventually regained most of his losses after the war ended, and died a citizen of Canada.

Although the Mount Allan location was not developed until 1947, the northern site developed by his European backers still bears the name "Nordegg."

Lillian Lake

the opposite side. A junction near the far side of the bridge links Terrace Trail with Galatea Creek. Turn left at this junction and begin climbing slowly up the valley. The trail zigzags over the creek several times in the next few kilometres until it stabilizes on the right hand side of the river. As it passes the steep slopes of Mount Kidd, it traverses a large avalanche slope hosting tasty plants for grizzlies in the spring. On busy weekends there are plenty of other hikers, and the likelihood of seeing master bruin is slim. Still, it wouldn't hurt to make some noise while crossing these slopes. The trail stays very wet until well into the hiking season. To reduce erosion, the trail is closed until around the third week in June each year. The actual date varies with the trail condition.

As you reach the upper end of the valley, the climbing be-

comes more steep for the final push towards Lillian Lake. The lakes are well known for their rainbow trout, so don't forget your license and fishing rod.

6. Centennial Ridge Trail

Are you ready for adventure? If so, then this is the trail for you. Climbing almost straight up the side of Mount Allan, this trail traverses the summit of the mountain at the 2,819-m (9,303-ft.) mark, making it the highest hiking trail in the Canadian Rockies. The trail is 11 km (6.6 mi.) to the summit, with an elevation gain of 1,355 m (4,480 ft.).

To ensure the trail has dried each spring, the route is closed between April 1 and June 22. Beginning at the Ribbon Creek parking lot, the first kilometre is gentle. The old coal mine scar on the side of the mountain heralds the beginning of the steep push. The

stretch ahead climbs 762 m (2,500 ft.) in less than 2 km (1.2 mi.). It's time to dig in and go for it. The footing is difficult due to the extreme steepness, but before you know it you'll be puffing on top of the Olympic platter. Beneath you was the start of the men's downhill during the 1988 games.

From the summit of the platter it is a constant, but more reasonable, climb along a ridge to the true summit. Along the way you'll pass the Rock Garden, a curious collection of rocky sentinels. These hard outcrops of conglomerate are more resistant to erosion and stand in defiance of the elements. At the summit there is a small cairn with a guest register. You might as well sign your name to prove you endured. The views are unobstructed in all directions. You can see Lac Des Arcs to the north and the steep faces of Mount Kidd block the southern skyline. To the west, Mounts Lougheed and Sparrowhawk are dominant.

From the summit most hikers return to Ribbon Creek, but if you are able to arrange a pick-up at the Alpine Resort Haven, near Dead Man's Flats, you can drop off the summit and descend back into the trees to make your way to the north trailhead.

7. Ptarmigan Cirque

Climbing high above Highwood Pass, the 5-km (3-mi.), self-guided loop of Ptarmigan Cirque provides a wonderful way to access the alpine. Park at the Highwood Pass parking lot and follow the signs towards the trail. It crosses Highway 40 and traverses forests of alpine larch, subalpine fir, and Engelmann spruce. Before you know it the views begin to open up.

The trail passes a large avalanche slope, whose lush growth testifies to the power of sunlight. With the trees removed, the area explodes with diverse plant life. This variety makes avalanche slopes prime habitat for many of our high-altitude residents. These include grizzly bear, elk, and bighorn sheep.

Beyond the avalanche slope, the trees begin to look stunted. The effects of altitude

Pika Paradise

THE PIKA IS one of the most amazing residents of the alpine. If you've never seen one, relax, you're not alone. Generally found only in desolate debris slopes, they blend perfectly with their rocky surroundings. Often, the first sign of a pika (pronounced "pee-kuh") is its strange call. It's this call that gives the animal its name, and it can be described as a sort of bleating "Peeek."

The sound generally comes from the middle of a seemingly lifeless rock slide, and before long it becomes a chorus that surrounds you. This is complicated by the nature of the rock slope, which causes the sound of a single call to seems like it comes from all directions—almost like a ventriloquist throwing his voice. This works very well to confuse predators.

Usually your first sighting begins with a flash of movement out of the corner of your eye. Upon further examination,

Pika

you'll find a small grey animal that resembles a guinea pig and blends in so well with the limestone that you'll almost lose it in the rocks. It is about 18 cm (7 in.) long, with short, rounded ears and no visible tail.

Pikas are not rodents, but are actually part of the rabbit family. Their body temperature is quite high, around 40°C (104°F), and a rise of between four and six degrees can be fatal. This narrow

Pika tracks

range forces them to live in cooler areas, usually at elevations above 2,100 m (6,930 ft.).

Unlike most other small members of the alpine community, the pika does not hibernate. It spends most of the summer months collecting plants and building large hay piles (some of which may be as large as a bushel) and leaving them to season, much like a farmer leaving out his bales. These stores will feed it through the eight or nine months of winter.

To collect its supply of plants, it must leave the security of its rock or talus slope. Recognizing its vulnerability, it spends as little time in the meadow as possible. Quickly gathering plants, it places them crossways in its mouth and returns to the talus.

There are many great spots to view pikas, but Rock Glacier is the very best I have ever found. Bring along your binoculars and your patience, as they are not easy to spot. It is definitely worth the effort.

The "Rock Garden" along the Mount Allan Centennial Trail

take over, and before long you leave the trees behind and move into the true alpine. Low shrubs and wildflowers reflect the harshness of this landscape. Keep your eyes open for ptarmigan wandering through the meadows. At the base of the bowl a small waterfall drains the seemingly endless supply of snow melt, and the straight-walled valleys above you are evidence of the former glaciers that sculpted them.

8. Cataract Creek

The forestry access roads along Cataract Creek allow easy access into remote country. Beginning along its lazy namesake creek, the wide route is used by hikers, horseback riders, mountain bikers, and, in winter, snowmobilers.

The first 6 km (3.6 mi.) have been upgraded in recent years to provide access to recent logging in the Lost Creek area. The views to the west, towards the High Rock Range, are wide open for much of this trail. Beyond Lost Creek, the route becomes more rustic as it begins to climb towards the head of the valley.

Higher up the valley you pass Perkinson's Cabin. This cabin was used by range riders. In days gone by they stayed with the cattle as summer custodians. The cabin has seen better days.

As the trail approaches Rye Ridge, at kilometre 19.1 (mile 11.5), the western skyline is blocked by a solid wall of mountains—the High Rock Range. On the opposite side of this barrier is the Province of British Columbia.

9. Etherington Creek

Located north of Cataract Creek, Etherington has a less-travelled character, but still traverses good-quality logging road. It begins gently, following former logging roads along Etherington Creek towards excellent views of the High Rock Range. It is best saved for mountain bikers and winter snowmobilers, as it has little in the way of scenery for hikers. It can be cycled in a loop by ascending Cataract Creek, crossing Rye Ridge, and then descending along Etherington Creek.

At one point, the trail vanishes. Floods in the spring of 1995 destroyed a short section. Cross the creek and, after a short upstream bushwhack, you can follow a dry runoff channel and find the trail before long.

As you reach the western end of the valley, the trail climbs hard and fast. It is a grueling climb if you're pushing a bike, but the views from the summit of the distant High Rock Range are a good inducement to continue. When you do reach the ridge, take a load off and enjoy the fruits of your labour.

6. Peter Lougheed Provincial Park

The Kananaskis Lakes from Opal Range

K ananaskis Provincial Park, as Peter Lougheed Provincial Park was originally known, was dedicated on September 22, 1977. One of the largest Provincial Parks in Alberta, it encompasses 304 sq. km (122 sq. mi.) around the Kananaskis Lakes. The park was created as part of the much larger Kananaskis Country. More than 20,000 people travelled to the park in its inaugural year, and things have been on an uphill swing since then.

The Kananaskis Lakes Trail takes you to the Upper and Lower lakes and past most of the facilities of Peter Lougheed Provincial Park. As one of the busiest corridors in Kananaskis, its 16 km (9.6 mi.) often seems like an urban jungle. Cyclists breeze along the paved bicycle path, hikers head into the backcountry, and mountain bikers grunt their way towards the top of one more hill—the valley pro-vides something for everyone. With some of the most picturesque landscape in all of Kananaskis, it begs to be explored.

Kananaskis Visitor Centre

During the early days of Kananaskis Country, money was plentiful and no expense was spared. Things have changed today, with cutbacks and deficits, but the legacy of this early period of prosperity can be seen in the quality of facilities located in Kananaskis. This attention to detail can be clearly seen in the Kananaskis Visitor Centre.

An abundance of slide shows and displays keep visitors busy for quite some time. The focus here is on interaction. Many of the displays require some form of input from the viewer, and several laser-disk programs provide high-tech access to trail information.

The staff at the Kananaskis Visitor Centre are experts on the area, and are an excellent source of information on current trail conditions and campground availability.

Beyond the desk a large sitting room with immense windows provides views of the surrounding Opal Ranges. With a roaring fire in the fire-

Opposite: Mount Burstall

place and extensive seating, it's the perfect place to warm up after a cold winter ski, or just relax after a summer hike. The centre can be contacted by calling (403) 591-7222.

William Watson Lodge

Every once in a while someone designs a facility that is so unique that it deserves accolades. William Watson Lodge is such a facility. Kananaskis Country has built a lodge

specifically for guests with physical and mental challenges. This provides opportunities to experience the splendour of Kananaskis in a barrier-free environment. The development includes eight specially-designed cabins and a main lodge. Guests don't need to restrict themselves to the cabins; there is also a barrier-free campground adjacent to the lodge. It accommodates six units and provides equally-accessible walk-in tent sites.

The lodge commemorates William Watson, a man who spent his life trying to improve the lives of disabled persons. He was born in 1904 in Scotland, and due to an injury at birth, spent his life without the use of his arms. Not one to give up, he still managed to earn a Bachelor of Arts degree and, later, a Bachelor of Laws, both from the University of Alberta. His handicap prevented him from practicing law, so he devoted his life to empowering

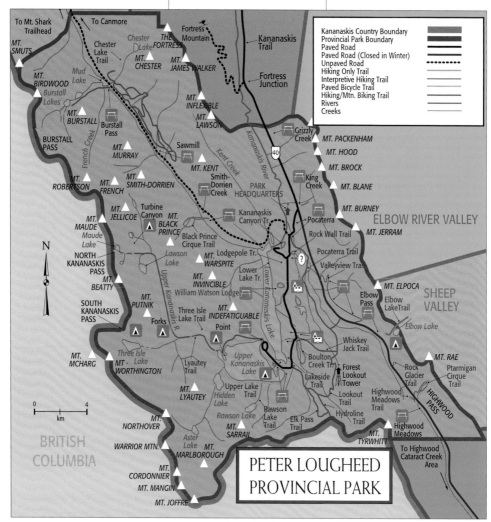

Lower Kananaskis Lake and the Opal Range

the disabled. He helped lay much of the groundwork for today's greater acceptance of persons with disabilities.

This facility is designed to be used by anybody with a physical or mental challenge. It doesn't provide attendants, but an eligible person may book a lodge for up to six people, and stay with them to provide assistance.

Surrounding the lodge there are numerous trails that are accessible to wheelchairs. These include Spruce Road Audio Trail, Marl Lake Trail, Rockwall Trail, and the Highwood Meadows Interpretive trails. The paved bicycle path, which snakes its way along the Kananaskis Lakes Trail, also provides a pleasant stroll or roll. The Evan–Thomas paved bicycle path, farther north on Highway 40, is yet another option. Finally, don't forget Mount Lorette Ponds, designed to provide barrier-free put-and-take fishing.

When you consider all of these opportunities for enjoying Kananaskis, the value of this facility begins to really shine. Few wilderness preserves in North America provide a similar service, and the prices are very reasonable. As you can imagine, these facilities are exceedingly popular, so reservations need to be made well in advance by calling (403) 591-7227.

Cottages

Hidden along the shores of the Lower Kananaskis Lake are a series of cottages. The only private residences in Kananaskis Country, the cottagers have worked hard to protect their secret. Even the access road is camouflaged. It joins with the Kananaskis Lakes Trail as a loose gravel road, but follow it a short distance and it quickly becomes paved. As the road passes the cottages, it becomes evident that this is prime real estate. In

1961, 70 cottage lots were leased for the princely sum of $5 plus a $30 annual fee. The new leasees had two years to build a cottage, and before long there were 75 stretched out along the shoreline. The cottages vary from deluxe to rustic, as each resident finds his own way to appreciate the beauty of the location.

Kananaskis Lakes

How does one describe the Kananaskis Lakes? They are a perfect combination of mountain, magic, and man. When explorer John Palliser first laid eyes on them in 1858 he remarked:

> "We came upon a magnificent lake, hemmed in by mountains, and studded by numerous islets, very thickly wooded. This lake, about 4 miles long and 1-1/2 miles wide, receives waters from the glacier above, and is a

87

Upper Kananaskis Lake in winter

Upper Kananaskis Lake in summer

favourite place of resort to the Kootenie Indians."

The two lakes are joined artificially through a penstock, a long pipe-like canal built between 1947 and 1955. Prior to this diversion, the lakes were linked by a small stream and waterfall.

George Pocaterra later described the changes brought about by hydro development.

"The most beautiful scenery in the world, as far as I am concerned, was at these lakes but now is completely spoiled by the power dams, the drowning of the marvelously beautiful islands and exquisitely carved beaches, the cutting down of the centuries old trees, and the drying up of the twin falls between the two lakes, and the falls below the lower lake."

The lakes provide numerous opportunities to hike, mountain bike, or fish. In 1994 the Lower Kananaskis Lake was stocked in August with 84,300 cutthroat trout, and the Upper in both August and September with 43,800 rainbow trout. Boat launches are provided at the Upper Lakes day use for access to the Upper Lake, and at Canyon day use for access to the Lower Lake.

Pocaterra

GEORGE POCATERRA was one of this area's most colourful, yet lesser-known pioneers. Born in Rocchette, Italy in 1883, he spent many years trapping and exploring the area now known as Kananaskis.

When he arrived on Canadian shores in 1903, he had $3.75, and began working on a small farm in Southern Manitoba. In the fall of 1904, the banks of the Highwood River became home, as he began work on what would eventually become one of the area's first "Dude Ranches"—the Buffalo Head Ranch. Soon he encountered his first "real" Indians, and this chance encounter led to a lifelong friendship with the Stoney Indians. One of those he met that day, Three Buffalo Bulls, later took him as a son. His other son,

George Pocaterra in 1911

Spotted Wolf, became Pocaterra's blood brother.

George, Spotted Wolf, and another Stoney named Dog Nose ran a trapline up the Kananaskis Valley. After dividing up the territory, Pocaterra trapped the area around both lakes and along a small stream that now bears his name. The winter of 1906-07 became known as the "year of the blue snows"—the year that the Chinook did not come. Pocaterra and his Stoney companions had a harrowing winter, almost not escaping the frozen grasp of the Kananaskis valley. Despite this ordeal, Pocaterra continued to hunt and trap in the area for another 20 years. He also filed several mineral deposits, but was unable to stimulate development of the sites. Although he opposed the hydro developments in the Kananaskis, one of the dams, a creek, and a group camp still bear his name. He died in 1972 at the age of 89, but his name lives on in the Kananaskis.

King Creek and the Opal Range

Peter Lougheed Provincial Park Trails

1. Paved Trail

The trail that parallels the highway as it winds towards the lakes is one of the most popular trails in the valley. Linking Lodgepole, Wheeler, and Lakeside trails, it meanders from Pocaterra day use all the way to Mount Sarrail Campground. In this way, almost the entire Kananaskis Lakes area is accessible by bikes, wheelchairs, hiking boots, or cross-country skis. For families looking for a summer outing, this trail is ideal. Kids of all ages can mount their bikes or trikes and plug along beside mom and dad. It does get busy, however, so make sure kids have a helmet, and try to stay to the right hand side of the trail. Along the way, stop in at the Kananaskis Visitor Centre. The many displays, along with numerous movies, will answer most of your questions about the area.

During the winter, this series of trails provides an excellent beginner-level trail, with options to head off in a variety of directions. There is one expert-level hill just after you leave the Pocaterra Ski Hut. You'll climb it on the way out, and descend it on your way back.

2. Pocaterra

Taking its name from George Pocaterra, this trail follows Pocaterra Creek as it climbs towards the fire lookout. George Pocaterra prospected up this creek and placed numerous claim stakes on promising outcrops of coal. He was associated with the MacKay and Dippie Coal Company. None of the deposits was ever mined, but a surveyor later stumbled across one of his claim stakes and named the creek flowing past it, Pocaterra Creek.

The trail climbs gradually, passing several marshy areas and intersecting numerous other winter trails. It provides an excellent mountain-bike ride in summer, particularly when linked with some of the other park trails to form a loop. In winter this linear trail attracts beginner-level cross-country skiers.

3. Fire Lookout

There are numerous routes to the Kananaskis Fire Lookout. Whichever route you choose, the view from the summit is worth the work. It can be accessed summer or winter, by foot, ski, or mountain bike. It provides the scenic focal point for mountain biking within Peter Lougheed Provincial Park, as there is no better park view accessible by bike.

The most direct access begins at the Boulton Creek Trading Post. Follow the Whiskey Jack Trail as it climbs steeply for 4.5 km (2.7 mi.) to a junction with Pocaterra Trail. If you are on a bike, numerous drainage channels have been cut across this trail, and can be dangerous in the downhill direction. As you meet the T-intersection at the end of Whiskey Jack, head right to climb towards the fire lookout. The trail to the lookout is well marked, and turns off to the right in 0.5 km (0.3 mi.). From this final junction, the last 1.8 km (1.1 mi.) climbs 220 m (720

Mount Indefatigable from the Hydroline Trail

ft.) towards the summit viewpoint.

Please keep in mind that lookouts are not public buildings. The Alberta Forest Service asks that you don't approach them. You can enjoy the view without disturbing the lookout personnel. From this point, the valley to the

Power Generation

Schooner Island on Upper Kananaskis Lake in 1911—now inundated

IN 1912 Calgary Power sent a survey party to assess the Kananaskis Lakes for their potential for hydroelectric development. They had already built the Horseshoe Dam on the Bow River and would soon complete the Kananaskis Falls Power Plant at the confluence of the Kananaskis and Bow rivers. The Kananaskis Lakes were almost spared in 1914, when a representative of the federal Water Power branch, M.C. Hendry, released a report suggesting that the development would be far too expensive to warrant consideration.

Unfortunately for the Lakes, as technology improved, so did the ability to make marginal dams pay off, and in 1932 a hand-hewn spillway on the Upper Kananaskis Lake was begun. This first dam was a primitive affair, with water flow being controlled by manually pulling out logs at two-week intervals in the spring and fall. Although this raised the water level, and pro-

vided a storage capacity of approximately 44 billion litres (11 billion gallons), a second dam was built 10 years later to almost triple the capacity to 126 billion litres (33 billion gallons), an area of 868 ha (2,170 acres). In 1955, Interlakes Plant was completed, and the storage capacity of the Upper Lakes was finally used to generate electricity. The capacity was small—just 5,000 kW, with a head of 39 m (127 ft.).

Even the Lower Kananaskis Lake was not spared to the

hunger for increased power generation, and clearing for its reservoir began in 1954. The following year, the Pocaterra Plant came on line with a usable storage of 63 billion litres (16 billion gallons), and an area of 641 ha (1,603 acres). Its power-generating capacity was 14,900 kW and its head 63 m (207 ft.). This, the Interlakes Plant, and the Barrier Plant are operated by remote control from the town of Seebe.

Subalpine larch in their fall plumage

west is spread out at your feet. The Upper and Lower Lakes sit at the base of a wall of mountains. To the northwest, Mount Indefatigable stands defiantly like the battleship after whom it was named. Directly west, the imposing face of Mount Lyautey still harbours several glaciers and sits adjacent to the Continental Divide.

From the lookout, cyclists and expert skiers may want to continue over the summit and descend down to Elk Pass Trail. Hikers will likely wish to return along the same route. The summer trail is dark and wet and offers little to attract hikers.

4. Elk Lakes

Cresting the Continental Divide and hiking to several attractive lakes in British Columbia is the main attraction of this route. The route is used by hikers, mountain bikers, and cross-country skiers. The pass is reached at kilometre 5 (mile 3), while the main entrance to Elk Lakes Provincial Park is a further 4.5 km (2.7 mi.). Although the trail to the Continental Divide is a lacklustre summer trail, it is very enjoyable in winter. It climbs over a small knoll from the parking lot and then follows Fox Creek for part of its ascent towards the pass. Just before the pass, Elk Lakes trail joins the wide Hydroline Trail that you will follow into B.C. The pass is quite low, only 1,960 m (6,468 ft.). From kilometre 9.5 (mile 5.7), at the main entrance to the park, you can hike or ski along a narrow trail towards the lakes. The Elk Lakes are in a magical valley surrounded by glacier-studded peaks. Beyond the Upper Elk Lake, at the end of a long gravel outwash plain, Petain Waterfalls provides a final destination for the ardent adventurer.

5. Mount Indefatigable

If you hike only one trail in Kananaskis Country, make this the trail. It's steep and rocky, but the views are absolutely superb. Climbing high above the Upper and Lower Kananaskis lakes, it provides a panorama that is hard to beat. The trail is short, only 4.3 km (2.6 mi.) one way, but it climbs 487 m (1,600 ft.) in that short distance.

The trail begins at North Interlakes day use area at the end of the Kananaskis Lakes Trail. After crossing the dam separating the Upper and Lower Lakes, branch off to the right and head north through the trees. The forest is dark and dreary for a short while, but after crossing a tiny bridge it climbs out of the trees and onto the exposed rock slope. The route along this ridge crosses some loose gravel, and you'll find yourself scrambling over numerous rocks, but the trail is well defined and the views keep improving with every step. Before you know it, you crest out on a ledge overlooking both lakes, and a seemingly out-of-place bench beckons you to take a load off. This is the scenic highlight of the trail, so take the time to do it justice. It is only a short distance, but you've done the most difficult part of the trail. As you continue climbing, the Upper Lake slowly disappears from view and the panorama begins to concentrate north, up the Lower Lake and the valley of the Smith–Dorrien/ Spray Trail. Near the upper extent of the trail, alpine larch show off their golden plumage each fall, making the trip worthwhile all over again.

It is tempting to keep going, climbing beyond the formal trail end, towards the various outliers of Mount Indefatigable. The mountain was named for a battleship at the Battle of Jutland in WWI, and, like a battleship, it is still taking casualties. In the summer of 1995, a hiker died while scrambling towards the summit. Scrambling is best reserved for very experienced hikers.

6. Three-Isle Lake

Of the backpacking routes in Peter Lougheed Provincial

Beaver Fever

PICTURE THIS. You're out hiking on one of Kananaskis Country's many hot summer days. You reach down into a pristine stream and splash a few handfuls on your face to cool down. A few weeks later you begin to notice an unpleasant change. It begins with a little diarrhea and progresses to include abdominal cramps, nausea, loss of appetite, weight loss, bloating, and abnormal amounts of gas. Chances are you've been chosen as a host for a tiny, single-celled animal known as *Giardia* ("gee-ARD-ee-uh") *lamblia*. This tiny parasite causes a malady known as giardiasis, commonly referred to as "Beaver Fever."

Giardia are so small that more than 15,000 can fit on the head of a pin, but it only takes a dozen or so to bring on giardiasis. Once ingested, they make their

Don't blame it on the beaver

way to your small intestine and eventually leave your body, hidden within cysts, in your wastes. In a full-blown case of giardiasis, you may excrete hundreds of millions of cysts per day.

The cure involves a few-weeks-worth of the drug Flagyl. This bombards your intestinal tract with chemicals designed to kill *Giardia*.

While it is true that beaver do carry the disease, so do many other animals, including man. Man must take some of the responsibility for the recent spread of this disease into more and more areas. Poor sanitary practices and the inclusion of "man's best friend" in the outdoor experience have allowed *Giardia* to move into areas not frequented by beaver. Dogs are even less particular than some hikers about where they do their business.

Proper treatment of drinking water can help make sure the little guys are not allowed into your intestines. There seems to be some dispute as to the effectiveness of various chemical treatments, so the two best remedies remain boiling for at least five minutes, or filtration. You will need a filter capable of filtering *Giardia* as small as 10–20 microns across.

Mount Sarrail and Upper Kananaskis Lake

Park, the route to Three-Isle Lake and the South Kananaskis Pass is by far the most popular. Beginning at North Interlakes day use, the trail follows the shoreline for 1.1 km (0.7 mi.) before branching off the main trail to the right. As it passes the base of Mount Indefatigable, it traverses a wooded valley to Forks campground at kilometre 8 (mile 4.8). This campsite forms a major backcountry junction. To the north lies Turbine Canyon (see next description), while to the west Three-Isle Lake and the South Kananaskis Pass beckon.

Beyond Forks the trail becomes markedly steeper. Up to this point it has remained fairly level, almost tedious. The change is rapid as it climbs the headwall towards the lake. From Forks, at approximately 1,753 m (5,785 ft.), it climbs to 2,173 m (7,171 ft.) at the lake—with the most elevation in the final 1.0 km (0.6 mi.). From the campsite, the South Kananaskis Pass is a final 2 km (1.2 mi.) with a moderate climb just before the summit.

7. Maude and Lawson Lakes

Turbine Canyon likely welcomed the first white travellers to the Kananaskis Valley in 1854 and provides some of the most elegant backpacking in the park. The trail begins along the same route as Three-Isle Lake. However, at Forks Campground, at kilometre 8 (mile 4.8), the route heads north, up the valley of the Upper Kananaskis River. This wide, glacial valley leads the hiker into an alpine wonderland, with numerous options for exploration.

When James Sinclair travelled this route in 1854, with 15 white families, 100 Cree, and 250 cattle, the route was so difficult the cattle had to be slaughtered. Sinclair describes a harrowing expedition, but he was the first white man to see the rugged Kananaskis valley.

Beyond Forks, the Maude–Lawson trail climbs steeply up the lower slopes of Mount Putnik. It eventually levels out along the base of Mount Beatty. Lawson Lake, with the Haig Glacier visible farther up the valley, is reached at kilometre 15 (mile 9). A short distance beyond, Turbine Canyon campground, along with a short spur trail to the canyon itself, is reached. A final 2 km (1.2 mi.) brings you past the desolate shores of Maude Lake, to the North Kananaskis Pass.

7. The Smith-Dorrien/Spray Trail

Chester Lake

This 60-km (36-mi.) road links the Kananaskis Lakes and the town of Canmore. Unpaved and exceedingly dusty in dry weather, its virtues far outweigh these relatively minor inconveniences. Combining travel beneath the glacier-scoured peaks of the Spray Mountains and the Goat Range with the picturesque shoreline of the Spray Lakes Reservoir, it is a splendid alternate route.

Also located along its length are numerous hiking and mountain-bike trails and a remote, but pleasant, campground.

The southern end of the road was little more than a forestry trunk road hacked out of the wilderness around 1936 and ending at the Mud Lakes area. The northern end of the road wasn't developed until hunger for hydro power in 1951 prompted construction of a steep road from Canmore to the newly created Spray Lakes Reservoir. The valley was logged by Spray Lake Sawmills in the 1950s. The highway has been dramatically upgraded since Kananaskis Country's inception, and now boasts a wide gravel surface along the southern 49 km (29 mi.), while the northern end remains narrow and winding. The drop down to Canmore also requires some confidence, as you drive along a steep mountain traverse, but the views during the descent are well worth it.

Gypsum Mine

On the steep slopes of Mount Indefatigable you may notice a faint diagonal line trending up the side and cutting through the trees near the summit. This cutline is all that remains of a gypsum mine attempted atop this remote mountain.

In 1964, a report published by the Geological Survey indicated deposits of gypsum along the north slope of Mount Indefatigable. Almost as soon as the report hit the presses, the Canadian Pacific Oil and Gas company applied for a permit. In 1965, it received a 21-year lease for the site. The lease was subsequently assigned to Alberta Gypsum.

The difficulties of building

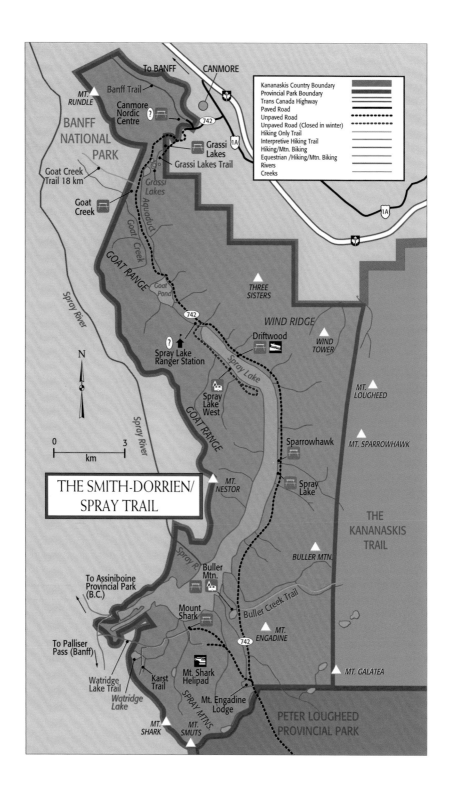

THE SMITH-DORRIEN/
SPRAY TRAIL

Kananaskis Country Boundary	
Provincial Park Boundary	
Trans Canada Highway	
Paved Road	
Unpaved Road	
Unpaved Road (Closed in winter)	
Hiking Only Trail	
Interpretive Hiking Trail	
Hiking/Mtn. Biking	
Equestrian /Hiking/Mtn. Biking	
Rivers	
Creeks	

Mount Shark

a road to the site proved nearly insurmountable. The first road came close, before reaching an impassable point. A second road was built along the northern side of Mount Indefatigable, the road still visible traversing this steep face.

Despite all this effort the deposit was of poor commercial quality, and only one carload of gypsum was ever taken out. In 1970, when Alberta Gypsum failed to pay for land restoration on the site, their lease was cancelled. With the advent of Kananaskis Country, mining was forbidden within its boundaries. Today the deposit remains where it lies, high on the slopes of Mount Indefatigable.

Mount Engadine Lodge

This splendid wilderness lodge was built in 1986 by Rudi and Elizabeth Kranabitter and Eric and Dorle Lomas. It provides the only lodge-style accommodation along this wilderness corridor, and is located at the junction of the Smith–Dorrien and Mount Shark roads. To the south, the three-peaked summit of Mount Birdwood dominates the skyline, and Mount Shark looms to the west. The lodge takes its name from Mount Engadine to the east, which in turn commemorates a light battle cruiser engaged in the Battle of Jutland during World War I.

Pleasantly rustic, it boasts a common sitting room with a large stone fireplace, a large dining area with plentiful European cuisine, and quiet rooms exuding simple luxury. From the lodge, a variety of exploring options are possible. Track-set cross-country ski trails lead out from the lodge,

hiking trails are located close by, and certified mountain guides are able to take you up the surrounding mountains. Options include simple accommodation packages and week-long adventure tours.

Mount Shark

The Canmore Nordic Centre lies in the Bow Valley and may not receive significant amounts of snow during the early part of the cross-country ski season. To ensure early- and late-season racing options, the Mount Shark ski trail system was designed. A former logging road provides easy access, and the trails provide a series of loops throughout this former clear-cut. The views down the valley towards the Spray Lakes Reservoir are attractive, and the network of trails challenging.

The trail system includes

Mud Lake

2-km, 5-km, 10-km and 15-km racing trails (1.2, 3, 6, and 9 mi. respectively) as well as the Ruedi Setz biathlon range. Ruedi was a former racer and a pivotal figure in the growth of biathlon in Alberta. He provided much of the impetus for the building of this facility.

Mount Shark also forms the main access point to Mount Assiniboine Provincial Park. The road to the trailhead passes a helipad, allowing for more leisurely access, whereas the main trail is used by hikers, mountain bikers, horseback riders, and skiers.

Mount Assiniboine

Shortly after passing the Mount Shark Road, you'll pass a small pond on the western side of the highway. Looking across Buller Pond, as it is known, you can see the towering wall of Mount Assiniboine. This mountain has captured the dreams of many travellers to the mountains. Walter Wilcox, who unsuccessfully attempted climbing the mountain in 1899, described it reflected in Lake Magog at its base:

Mt. Assiniboine

> *The majestic mountain, which is a noble pyramid of rock towering above snow fields, was clearly reflected in the water surface. Such a picture so suddenly revealed aroused the utmost enthusiasm of all our party, and unconsciously everyone paused in admiration.*

It was named in 1884 by surveyor George Dawson after the Stoney Indians of the Assiniboine nation. Assiniboine loosely translates to "stone boiler." Prior to the introduction of metal cook pots, the Stoneys would heat rocks and place them into cooking receptacles, thus heating water to cook their food.

The mountain is often referred to as the "Matterhorn of the Rockies." Its craggy summit has been carved by glacial ice on four sides, giving it a striking similarity to its European namesake. It rises 3,618 m (11,870 ft.) and is visible from very few areas in the Kananaskis. This sight is a special treat on clear days.

Mount Sparrowhawk

High above Sparrowhawk day use area are the towering slopes of its namesake mountain. This site has seen numerous failed proposals to develop a world-class ski resort. As early as 1970, developers were trying to coax approval from a reluctant Alberta Government. The attempts were politely rejected, but the proposals continued to come. In 1978, a group called the Spray Lakes Ski Corporation submitted a $300-million develop-

Mount Nestor and Spray Lakes Reservoir

ment proposal. It was tentatively approved, but, following an election, subsequently turned down as being too grandiose.

The proposal was scaled down to a more manageable $50 million, again rejected and again scaled down. Even the modest $25-million development finally proposed would have supported 5,000 to 8,000 skiers a day.

During this same period there was speculation that this site could double as the host site for the downhill events of the 1988 Winter Olympics. The Calgary Olympic proposals for the games used Sparrowhawk as the mountain of choice. It could easily provide the 300-m (1,000-ft.) vertical drop necessary for an Olympic event.

In the end the mountain was rejected. Mount Allan was chosen for the 1988 games, and the proposal for a ski resort was turned down. To date, Mount Sparrowhawk remains

the sole domain of mountain goats and mountain climbers, not to mention a few intrepid scramblers clambering for the rocky summit.

Spray Lakes

The Spray Lakes began as a small series of mountain lakes enhanced to provide hydroelectric power. To this end, it puts the capabilities of the Kananaskis Lakes to shame. As early as the 1920s, negotiations with the federal government over the status of the lakes were being undertaken. At that time, they were within the boundaries of Rocky Mountains Park, now Banff. The park was much larger then, and included Canmore, the Spray Lakes, and Lac Des Arcs within its boundaries. In 1928, the Department of the Interior agreed to remove Spray Lakes from the Park if the province would guarantee a flow of 350 second-feet down the Spray River to Banff. The

Crag and Canyon Newspaper, on December 10, 1928, described the Spray Lakes as:

"A valley full of muskeg…and old burnt stumps, the largest slope of the Canadian Rockies, that breeds uncountable numbers of mosquitoes, and flies. Surely a place to clean up, and what more fitting way than to submerge it in a big lake, where the natural sloping of the ground and feeding place, will increase the fast vanishing fishing of the Spray Lake…

Spray Lakes sports a fish rarely caught anywhere else in the mountains. All these trout weigh close to four pounds each and time and again it has been said, by fishermen who know the streams of Europe, that they never

103

had better sport than what they got from Spray Lakes, so that with the raising of Spray Lakes, these fish would be preserved indefinitely and mean an income to all the Dominion."

The Spray System finally came on line in 1951, and is composed of three power plants and several dams. Spray Lakes is formed by Canyon and Three Sisters dams. Together, they create a reservoir 1,987 ha (4,968 acres) in size, with a storage capacity of 421,850,000 m^3 (18 trillion $ft.^3$). This makes it larger than the combined capacity of the Up-per and Lower Kananaskis lakes, and Barrier Lake. Canyon Dam is located at the southwestern end of Spray Lakes, where the Spray River enters the lake. Three Sisters Dam keeps the water contained at the northern end. After leaving Three Sisters Dam, the water drops 20 m (66 ft.) to

Canmore Nordic Centre

CANMORE BECAME the host community for the cross-country and biathlon events for the 1988 Winter Olympics. Prior to this site being chosen as the official Olympic venue, other sites were also investigated. The old Pigeon Mountain ski area was one potential location for the Nordic events. Other hopeful sites included the Paskapoo Ski area (now Canada Olympic Park) in Calgary, and the community of Bragg Creek. Although Bragg Creek had been used in the original Olympic proposals, concerns over lack of snow resulted in its being removed from final consideration. In the end, it was between the Pigeon Mountain site and Canmore. Although Olympic officials expressed a preference for Pigeon Mountain, it was on private land, and the government wanted to avoid incurring the additional expense of purchasing land. In 1983, Canmore got the nod, and development began in earnest. Three years later, in August of 1986, the trail network was officially approved by Dietrich Martin, the technical representative for the 1988 games.

In the winter of 1987 the site was officially opened, and it hosted its first World Cup event. With the coming of the Olympics, the site was fenced in, and security

Cross-country skier

was high. When the athletes descended on Canmore, where they were housed in a specially designed residential complex, they quickly made their presence known. Colourful jerseys jogged along local roadways, and pin trading with athletes and visitors from all over the world became a way for non-athletes to get involved.

The events were a great success, and since that time the site has hosted a diversity of activities. From the Ziggy Gnarly Mountain Bike race to the annual Canmore Sled Dog Races, to regular World Cup cross-country and biathlon events—there is always something happening at the Nordic Centre.

Following the games, the site was converted into a year-round

Mountain bike racer

training centre. There is now a 2.5-km (1.5-mi.) paved trail to allow skiers to train with roller skis during summer. This same trail is lighted for night skiing during the short days of winter. Snow making on approximately 60% of the tracks ensures a reliable snow supply. There are also facilities for team use, as well as a weight room and meeting facilities.

In an attempt to cover some of the operating costs, user fees may be charged to winter skiers. In the winter of 1995-96, fees were implemented but quickly withdrawn after public outcry. It is likely they will reappear, perhaps at lower rates than originally proposed. For the time being, summer access will continue to be free.

Canmore lies beneath the imposing face of Mount Rundle

Three Sisters Power Plant. This drop is enough to generate only 3,000 kW, making it the smallest power plant operated by Trans Alta Utilities. Continuing through a series of canals, the water passes through Goat Pond on its way to Whiteman Dam and the Spray Power Plant. As it drops 274 m (904 ft.) from this dam, through a dual penstock, it generates an additional 102,800 kW. The final power plant in the Spray System is just west of Canmore, where the water drops a final 98 m (323 ft.) to join the Bow River at the Rundle Power Plant, and produces an additional 49,900 kW. The total energy production of the Spray System is 155,700 kW—enough to provide power to a city of 100,000 people. This generating system far surpasses the Kananaskis System's combined capacity of only 33,800 kW.

Penstock

As you drive past the White-man Dam Reservoir, you'll notice a large metal pipe dropping from the dam down into the valley. Built in 1960, this penstock, as it is called, carries water from the reservoir down a drop, or head, of 274 m (904 ft.). This is the largest drop in the Trans Alta system. At the base of this steep cliff, the water enters the Spray Power Plant, and the energy generated during the drop is used to turn the blades of several large turbines. This in turn generates hydroelectric power. This one penstock produces 52,900 kW of energy. Hidden within the mountain face is a second penstock, the original. It opened in 1951 with a capacity of 49,900 kW. The combination of the two generating units allows for the generation of 102,800 kW .

The metal penstock is the result of wartime technology. Prior to World War II, there were few metals strong enough to be used for external penstocks, so they were rou-tinely built into the hillsides. As more durable armaments were developed for battle, these technologies were used for more peaceful pursuits.

Town of Canmore

Dropping down the steep hill from Whiteman Dam, you get some spectacular views of the town of Canmore. Nestled along the lower slopes of Mount Rundle, in the shadow of the Three Sisters, it sits in a valley that begs to be explored.

Canmore is a town born of coal. Like many towns in Alberta, it began as little more than a mine site around which a community developed. Considering the pace at which it's growing, it's easy to forget these humble beginnings.

Coal was first reported by George Dawson while making the first major study of this area in 1885. Discovering quite a supply of coal, he named the formation the Cascade Coal Basin, and this coal seam stretched from north of Banff to south of Canmore. It was the Canadian Anthracite Company of Eau Claire, Wisconsin that opened up the mines in Canmore and Anthracite (west of Banff). They beat the Canadian Pacific Railway to the punch and were able to supply them with coal until they opened their own mine at Bankhead.

Of the three mines, Canmore's was the most viable. Its coal was much easier to remove because it was thicker and not as steeply bedded. Canmore's mine proved itself by operating until 1979, whereas Bankhead closed in 1922 and Anthracite lasted only a few years, closing in 1904.

If you'd like a taste of the past, take a walk on the Georgetown trail at the Nordic Centre, or drive up to the old site of Bankhead mine in Banff and walk the old townsite or the C-Level Cirque trail. You can still feel the history and see some of the old mine remnants. Also, don't miss the Canmore Centennial Museum as you pass through town. It highlights much of the town's history as a coal mining community.

Canmore is one of the fastest growing communities in Alberta. It contains a downtown full of pleasant coffee shops and galleries. Its hotels cater to visitors seeking a quieter experience than offered in busy Banff, and its businesses offer lower prices. Since the Olympics, its population has almost doubled. Today, tourism development is happening at a breakneck pace, and the town has instituted a Growth Management Strategy

Buller Pond with Mount Assiniboine in the distance

to help slow the town's rapid expansion. The town realizes the danger of compromising the very reason visitors flock to the mountains, and the next 10 years will largely define the future appearance of this mountain valley.

Spray Trails
1. Burstall Pass
This 7.5-km (4.5-mi.) trail is a favourite. It is easy to access and provides endless opportunities for wilderness wandering. From the pass, the view of the three-summited dogtooth

Glacial Nurseries

ALONG THE southern end of the Smith–Dorrien/Spray Trail, the western skyline is dominated by the glacially-carved faces of Mounts Invincible, Warspite, and Black Prince. Large bowl-like depressions have been carved into the mountain faces, and these bowls were once the birthplace of a glacier.

Mountain glaciers are formed by the slow accumulation of snow within a small depression. Later, as the depth of snow increases, the lower layers become compressed into ice. As the ice layers get thicker with each passing year, pressure on the lower layers causes them to flow, slowly, like a thick liquid. As ice moves within these alpine depressions, the glacier carves

out a large bowl, or cirque, before flowing into the surrounding valley.

Later, the ice disappears from most of these glacial bowls. Some were trapped in the bottom and later melted to become one of the many glacial lakes found in the Rockies. These cirque lakes are called tarns and are quite common within Kananaskis Country. Black Prince Trail takes you to one such tarn. In some instances, the water carved a channel through the bowl's lip, and formed a waterfall to the valley bottom. Ptarmigan Cirque on Highwood Pass shows this post-glacial carving—the water flows down Mounts Rae and Arathusa.

Mount Chester

peak of Mount Birdwood seems to hold the eyes indefinitely. To the west, Leman Lake and Mount Queen Elizabeth beckon. On the pass itself, wide open country allows ample exploration without any firm destination in mind. During winter, the Pass provides a challenging destination for advanced backcountry skiers looking for tempting slopes to telemark.

The trail begins rather modestly, with 3 km (1.8 mi.) of former logging road. This is a great place to bring along your mountain bike. You can take a little time off the approach and increase the time for playing at the pass. Along the road, three small lakes, one for each summit of Birdwood, are passed in rapid suc-

cession. They're just off the main trail—why not wander down to their picturesque shorelines? Mirror-like reflections of the mountains can be seen in their calm waters.

At the end of the logging road you cross a gravel wash, alive with tough yellow mountain avens. As you cross the flats, notice the snowy face of Roberston Glacier to the south. This inviting valley can be a death trap in winter, when avalanches thunder down one side and up the other. In summer it's another area to explore, but only a hiker-defined trail exists. Remember, glaciers are dangerous. Crevasses can be hidden by thin snow bridges, only to collapse as you walk over them. Travel on the ice is for experienced, well-equipped parties only. On the far side of the wash, the trail enters the trees and follows the stream towards the pass.

The trail climbs rapidly through the trees until it crests the lower part of the pass, providing a hint of the views to come. Back down the valley, Mounts Birdwood and Chester dominate. Up the valley, the pass awaits. In fall, plentiful

alpine larch turn it into a golden playground.

From the pass, you can look across the Spray valley to Leman Lake and the Royal Group of mountains. The wind whistles over this exposed ridge, so make sure you bring along a jacket to protect against its bite.

2. Chester Lake

This 5-km (3-mi.) trail combines a winding logging road with a pleasant single track, and culminates with a tiny lake beneath an imposing rock face. The road is not very impressive, as it switches back for the first few kilometres, but once you head into the woods you enter a pleasant subalpine world. As you approach the lake, the trail crosses a marshy meadow rimmed with alpine larch. Mount Chester's sheer face looks sternly down at the tiny lake, also called Chester.

This trail is equally pleasant in winter, when it makes a nice backcountry ski trip. It is not maintained, but usually is well packed by the large numbers of skiers heading up to the lake. Once in the trees, the skiing can be quite tight, especially on the way down. You need to be a confident tree skier to enjoy this downhill slalom.

The trail is well marked all the way, and Mount Chester makes an easy landmark should you wander off the beaten path. For those that like to wander off the trail, there are numerous exploration opportunities in the area.

3. Buller Pass

This 10.5-km (6.3-mi.) trail is an alternate access route to the Ribbon Creek area and

Mountain Goats and the Goat Range

ALONG THE SHORES of Spray Lakes Reservoir, the western sky is filled with the impressive faces of the Goat Range. Named after the mountain goat, an animal that eschews the valleys for the inhospitable alpine summits, it implies ruggedness, and it delivers. The south end of the range begins with Mount Nestor, named for a destroyer sunk at the Battle of Jutland.

Mountain goats are one of the most highly adapted of our mountain wildlife. No other animal has the ability to survive on the summits like goats. Even bighorn sheep, another well-known climber, defers to the mountain goat. Easily recognized by its white, shaggy coat and black goat-like horns, it is rarely seen along the roadways. Despite its name, it is actually related to the mountain antelope of Asia—it's not a goat at all!

Animals that stay white year-round are rare in nature, but the goat has found this to be an advantage. For most animals, a white coat in summer is too visible, making them vulnerable to predators. For the goat, though its white colour is clearly visible, it is often discounted as a patch of summer snow—that is, until it begins to move. Often you will see numerous goats in an area, and you may find collections of their pellets beneath rocky overhangs, which serve as shelters.

Even mountain goats sometimes fall, but more fall victim to the unpredictable na-

Mountain Goats

ture of avalanches. In winter they prefer the wind-blown summits, which keep sufficient grasses exposed for feeding. Ironically, when the hunt for food results in the release of an avalanche, they provide food for grizzlies. As these large eaters wake from their winter sleep, they head to the avalanche slopes to feed on the carcasses of winter-killed sheep and goats. The main predator of the mountain goat is the cougar, but the rocky crags provide protection from most non-human hunters.

Each spring, mountain goats shed their winter coats. This brings on a desire for salt, which may bring them down to the valley bottoms. Occasionally they appear along roadsides, where they lick glacial gravels that provide some of these minerals. Unfortunately, they are rarely seen at road

level in Kananaskis. In some areas in Kananaskis, mountain goats are being reintroduced: the Picklejar Lakes area south of Highwood Pass and near the summit of Nihahi Ridge in the Elbow River Valley. If successful, this program will allow their shaggy coats to be seen more widely within the boundaries of Kananaskis Country.

Karst Spring

panoramic views of the Spray Lakes Valley to the west. Climbing high above the Spray Valley, it provides access to an alpine pass. Here there are numerous opportunities for experienced scramblers. Finally, it descends into the valley of Ribbon Lake, where you can exit over Guinn's Pass or descend the Ribbon Creek Valley.

Beginning at Buller Mountain day use area, along the dusty Smith–Dorrien/Spray Trail, it quickly crosses the outlet of Buller Pond and heads up the valley of Buller Creek. Mounts Buller and Engadine form a narrow valley in which the trail winds. After a few stream crossings, the river forms a small waterfall as it pours over a resistant layer of rocks. Beneath the falls, the power of water is revealed in the round pool carved by the action of water constantly swirling around it.

The climbing becomes more gradual until it turns up the south Buller Creek drainage. After a moderate

kilometre, the trail begins to climb steeply towards the pass. The next kilometre will take you a final 250 m (825 ft.) to the summit of Buller Pass. Drink in the views, along with some of the water you wisely packed, and begin the descent down towards Ribbon Lake. After dropping about 335 m (1,106 ft.), you'll cross Upper Ribbon Creek and encounter the junction of the trails to Ribbon Lake and Guinn's Pass.

4. Mount Assiniboine Provincial Park via Mount Shark

How does one describe the route to Mount Assiniboine? This is an area that must be experienced to be believed. Although the main access is through Kananaskis Country, this route passes through parts of Kananaskis, as well as Banff National Park, before entering Mount Assiniboine Provincial Park in British Columbia. Culminating at Lake Magog, beneath the towering horn of Assiniboine, this trail should be near the top of anyone's list.

Winter and summer, the access to Assiniboine is varied. Options include horseback, helicopter, mountain bike, cross-country skis or even foot. The last two are by far the most difficult, requiring a backpack and gear for several days. More and more mountain bikers are heading into the park, and this has led to some concerns over impact. At present, you can ride your bike to Lake Magog over Assiniboine Pass, but no farther. From that point, if you wish to explore other areas of the park, you'll need to do it on foot. The distance from Mount Shark to Lake Magog tops out at 25.5 km (15.8 mi.).

The trail comprises a spin along Mount Shark and Bryant Creek trails, followed by a steep climb over Assiniboine Pass to 2,180 m (7,152 ft.), before dropping down to Lake Magog. As an out-and-back trail, the total mileage for the day is 51 km (31.7 mi.). The trail condition varies from wide-open fire road to narrow, deeply rutted single track. Due to the remoteness, elevation gain, and long distance to be covered, this trail is rated for expert bikers.

Accommodation at the lake is varied. At one extreme you can go in style and stay at Assiniboine Lodge, a privately operated wilderness lodge near Lake Magog. At the other extreme are numerous campsites within Mount Assiniboine Provincial Park. Right in the middle, and generally just right, are the Naiset Cabins. Operated by the park, they are simple cabins with wood stoves for heat. They provide excellent winter camping op-

Goat Pond and the Goat Range

portunities, and are worth utilizing. They are operated on a first-come, first-served basis during the summer, but in winter, reservations are required to ensure space. Reservations can be made by calling (604) 422-3212 or by mail to B.C. Parks, Box 118, Wasa, B.C., V0B 2K0.

5. Karst Trail

This pleasant trail can be a destination of its own, or a short diversion when travelling towards Mount Assiniboine via the Watridge Lake trail. Following the trail to the lake, Karst is a 0.8-km (0.5-mi.) side trip that takes you through the woods along a brilliant-green, moss-carpeted spring. Following the Karst trail, you leave the lakeshore and head into the woods, staying to the right side of the stream. Along the upper extent of the trail a wooden boardwalk allows you to move around a resistant rock outcrop and witness the source of the stream—a spring bursting

forth from the rock face itself.

6. Goat Creek

This trail is one of the most popular summer mountain bike and winter cross-country ski routes in the Rockies. Providing easy access to Banff, its 18 km (10.8 mi.) take the rider along the backside of Mount Rundle. For hiking, there are other options that offer more in the way of scenery, and you don't reach any alpine vantage points on this trail, but it is a nice route to explore.

Mountain-bike riders of all abilities will enjoy this trail, as it is perfect for introducing novices to the sport, but, at the same time, it gives expert riders some exhilarating opportunities for quick downhill rides. Have a vehicle drop you off at the trailhead, otherwise you will need to climb a steep, dusty, 7.7-km (4.8-mi.) gravel road rising 366 m (1,200 ft.) to access the trail.

Beginning on the Spray Lakes Road, high above the community of Canmore, the

ride is almost entirely downhill, dropping from an elevation of 1,675 m (5,495 ft.) down to the elevation of Banff, at 1,384 m (4,538 ft.).

The scenery is pleasant, though not spectacular, along this ride. Paralleling the length of Mount Rundle, you are treated to numerous views of its steeply bedded slopes. This mountain, one of the most photographed in the Rockies, is a classic example of a Front Range peak. Although more of a range than a single peak, it exhibits rock layers thrust up at steep angles. It gains its name from one of the first white men to set foot in this area way back in 1845. Reverend Robert T. Rundle was a Methodist Missionary who worked extensively with the local Stoney Indians. On numerous occasions, the trail does well-bridged stream crossings as it follows Goat Creek and, later, the Spray River. Thus the sound of water is a common and pleasant

Grassi Lakes

Pictograph

addition to this ride.

7. Grassi Lakes

This short trail is only 1.8 km (1.1 mi.) each way, but is a trail that everyone should walk at least once. The trailhead is at the start of the Smith–Dorrien/Spray hill, along a signed access road veering to the east. There are many trails within Kananaskis Country, but this one holds a special fascina-

tion. It has a combination of colour, water, and history.

The trail begins simply with a stroll along a closed access road, but quickly leaves the road along a single track to the left. Winding through a lodgepole pine forest, you soon begin to hear water flowing. As the trail begins to climb, you get some dramatic views of a waterfall coming

down from the pass high above. Forming a ribbon of water, it also signals a steep climb, up a long series of stone steps, to the trails junction with the lakes themselves.

Named after trail-builder Lawrence Grassi, these lakes provide a colour rarely seen in the mountains. A deep, almost fluorescent blue, the ponds are bound on one side by a steep cliff face. This ancient coral reef is full of evidence of its marine origins. To the left of the upper lake, a loose scree slope takes the intrepid explorer farther up the valley to view Indian pictographs that may be hundreds of years old. A quick exit can be had by following the road all the way from the lakes to the main trailhead parking lot.

8. Bow Valley Provincial Park

Mount Yamnuska

Found along the Trans Canada Highway, Bow Valley Provincial Park provides a unique combination of Aspen Parkland and plains, sitting at the base of Mount Yamnuska. It explodes into a yellow-green colour each May, as the aspen leaves burst out of their winter buds. The valley seems to breathe a sigh of relief as the colours change from the drab brown of winter to the wonderful greens of summer. Even before the leaves appear, wildflowers like the prairie crocus add their pink flowers to the landscape.

During the final advance of glacial ice, known as the Canmore Advance, the Bow Valley Glacier reached only to present-day Bow Valley Provincial Park. To the east, the huge continental ice sheet also petered out before reaching this location. Numerous landforms in the park area testify to the terminal position of the ice. As ice retreated, it left behind depositional landforms and numerous kettle lakes. Kettles form when huge blocks of ice are buried under glacial debris. When the ice later melts, it creates a meltwater pond. This is how some of the park lakes originated.

Today the facilities in the park include numerous campsites, along with several pleasant interpretive trails. The easy access to the highway makes it a perfect staging area for day trips into the surrounding valleys. After all, the park sits in an ancient travel corridor that hosted visitors for more than 10,000 years.

Bow Valley Park Trails

1. Flowing Water Interpretive Trail

From Willow Rock Campground, this 1.4-km (.9-mi.) self-guided trail describes the power of water as it takes you along the Kananaskis River, and past a small beaver pond. On the way, the trail crosses an iron-rich stream, and wanders along a bench above the river for about half its length. The views down the winding Kananaskis River are quite open here, and occasionally you can see whitewater rafters or paddlers plying the swift waters of the river. Beyond the

Opposite: Trembling aspens

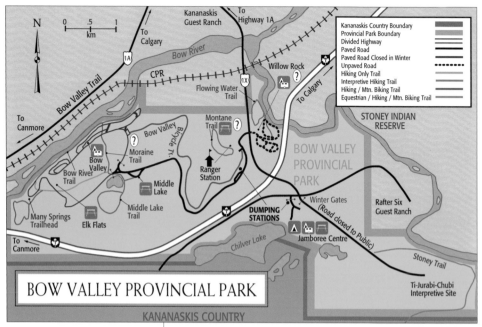

BOW VALLEY PROVINCIAL PARK

KANANASKIS COUNTRY

river, it climbs a glacial ridge and provides excellent views of the surrounding peaks. It finishes by passing through several wetlands, rich with evidence of beaver.

2. Montane Trail

Located behind the information centre, the Montane Trail takes you past a wildflower-laden meadow, traverses a forest of aspen, and follows a forest of Douglas fir before returning to the visitor centre. Along the route of this fairly level 2.2-km (1.3-mi.) trail, you pass numerous points of interest. The meadow behind the park office is an excellent place to look for some of the first wildflowers of spring. Often in early May the prairie crocus is poking its head through late snowfalls. Beyond, the trail passes a series of sinuous ridges known as eskers. Left behind by the Bow Valley Glacier, these are formed when tunnels within

World Scout Jamboree

IN 1983 Kananaskis Country was "invaded" by a force of 15,000 uniformed troops from 74 countries. Luckily, however, the troops were scouts, participants in the XV World Jamboree held in Bow Valley Provincial Park from July 6–16, 1983. The logistics for this event were mind-numbing. Ray Andrews of Kananaskis Country was the manager in charge of the event. He spent more than a year organizing staff and training leaders. The event was deemed a success by none other than Lord Baden Powell, the grandson of the movement's founder. The purpose of the event was to celebrate the diversity of world cultures. A miniature international village featured displays, exhibits, and foods from the countries represented.

The scouts didn't remain on site the whole time, but were

One of the many cultural displays

provided with trips to the many nearby attractions. Some visited the Columbia Icefields and others headed to the Calgary Stampede. How do you say "yahoo" in Bangladesh? Other scouts went whitewater rafting, hiking, and mountain climbing, not to mention western mainstays like roping, riding, and gold panning.

Mount Lougheed

the glacier become choked with debris. When the ice melts, this debris is deposited in linear ridges.

The trail takes its name from the remnant of Douglas fir forest that the trail passes. This tree indicates Montane forest. It survives well in wind-blasted sites like this. It has become less common over the years, as stands of ancient trees fall victim to the axe.

3. Bow Valley Bicycle Path

Like paved paths in other parts of Kananaskis, this sinuous route provides pleasant access from the Bow Valley Campground to the park's visitor centre. It winds through a mixture of open meadow and aspen and Douglas fir trees. Many of the aspen look stunted, a direct result of the high winds that prevail in this valley. The mountains lining the Bow Valley act like a wind funnel, and the trees at the entrance to the valley are the unlucky recipients of these forces.

Along the way, stop in one of the meadows and count the different types of flowers present. The Bow Valley Visitor Centre can help you with questions you may have on identification, or see if you can find a few from this book. While the trail is tame, please wear a helmet whenever riding your bike.

4. Middle Lake

Shhh! Hiking the shores of Middle Lake is a good place to stay very quiet and watch for some of the plentiful birdlife of this slough pond. The lake is fed by underground springs and surface runoff, so it has no river source. There are no fish to catch, but the birdlife is diverse. Red-necked and horned grebes can be seen swimming in the water, while redwing blackbirds perch atop the reeds.

The trail is signed in a clockwise direction, taking you along the shoreline first. During June the trail hosts large numbers of western wood lilies. Be careful if you stop to sniff them. They tend to deposit dark brown pollen on the tip of your nose if you get too close—and of course nobody will tell you how silly you look. As you travel the loop, you'll see numerous Douglas fir stumps, left behind during logging operations of the Eau Claire logging company. If you're lucky, you may get to see some of the elk that make the park home; if not, you do get to see the signs of one of the other park residents—the black bear. The trail passes some trees scarred by the action of black bears climbing. Aspen trees hold such scars for life, as their bark is easily marked.

5. Many Springs Trail

This should be one of the first trails to head for within Bow Valley Park, especially if you like wildflowers. Many of the other trails provide a plethora of colourful flowers, but none can compete with the diversity found along this short trail. The self-guided route circumnavigates a tiny spring-fed slough. The trail circles the springs in a counter-clockwise direction, past western wood lilies, in their peak flower season in early June. The trail makes its way around the pond to the far side, where boardwalks take you through a pleasant wetlands. On the margins of the water, a seemingly endless variety of flowers bloom. The pink elephants head stands taller than most, but it's tiny flowers along the spike-like head that reveal the reason for its name. Lower down, delicate blue butterworts survive in the nitrogen-poor soils of the marsh by curling up their leaves and digesting unsuspecting insects that land on their sticky

Elk

Stag elk

BOW VALLEY PROVINCIAL PARK supports an elk herd of approximately 75 animals. Their tan coats and large antlers are easily identified. Each antler can weigh more than 12 kg (26 lbs.). Elk are grazers, and spend most of the summer munching on the grasses and flowers of the local meadows. Within the park the snow is often shallow due to the powerful Chinook winds. The elk paw through the snow to get at the grasses only a few inches below.

In years where the snows are deep, they may resort to chewing the bark of aspen trees. This contributes to the dark bark on the lower part of many such trees.

In the fall, the rut brings a little romance to the park. The stags are in peak condition, and the competition between them can be intense. Their strategies are based on a single male mating with as many cows as he can collect, and keep. The strongest male mates, and when the game is done, often so is he. He limps away, wilted and weak, just before the harsh winter. Needless to say, the reigning male changes regularly.

The calves appear in the spring, and the cows become very protective at this time. Don't approach a cow with a calf, as you may end up with a serious injury—elk are incredibly fast, and very strong.

Opposite: Heart Creek

Guest Ranches

Ever since ranching arrived in the foothills, guest ranches were destined to become a popular vacation option. The concept is simple—invite guests in to see life on a ranch. Offer them the opportunity to ride the range, and provide good food and rustic accommodation. Bow Valley Provincial Park is host to two separate ranches—the Kananaskis Guest Ranch and Rafter Six Ranch Resort.

Kananaskis Guest Ranch

When John and Isabella Brewster arrived in the Banff area in 1886, the whole nature of the valley changed. The Brewsters opened a dairy, and this humble start led to the building of an empire. During the winter, when business was slow, the family homesteaded beneath the face of Mount Yamnuska, at the site of the present ranch. Two of the sons, Bill and Jim, loved the wilderness and became insatiable explorers. When the Banff Springs Hotel asked them to guide a party of fishermen when they were at the tender ages of 12 and 10, they set in motion the beginnings of the Brewster Mountain Pack Trains Company. The two brothers also started the successful motor coach company that still bears the family name, but it was purchased by Greyhound Canada in 1965, leaving the family to concentrate on their guiding operations.

Over the years the ranch expanded. The main lodge was built in 1922. The1930s were difficult, but Bill's wife Sylvia (better known as "Missy") and her eldest son Claude kept things going. Claude's sons Jack and Bud in

turn took over the ranch. Bud added the famous Do-nut tent and the Lyster paddle wheeler seminar room in the 1960s. In 1987, more renovations were needed to keep pace with the times. Today, it is managed by a fifth generation of the Brewster family. With over 100 years of tradition behind them, the Brewster family welcomes you to the Kananaskis Guest Ranch. For more information call (403) 673-3737.

Rafter Six Ranch Resort

Rafter Six Ranch Resort sits south of the Trans Canada Highway, hidden from sight. As you pull up, past the chipmunk-crossing signs, the ranch suddenly looms into view, and you wonder how you could have missed it. In 1873 Colonel James Walker, a member of the Northwest Mounted Police, opened a sawmill on the site to supply the outpost at Fort Calgary. It was later acquired by a crusty curmudgeon known as Soapy Smith. After Smith died, his young wife Eva married Alvin Guinn, the son of a local rancher. In the 1930s they turned the site into a guest ranch. It grew slowly, but eventually

tents were replaced by log cabins. A main lodge was built, which includes the present dining room.

Hollywood discovered the location in the 1950s, and Marilyn Monroe was filmed at the site in "River of No Return." Later movies such as "Grizzly Adams," and "Across the Great Divide," also used the site. In 1994, the comedy "How the West Was Fun," was filmed here.

In 1978 the ranch was taken over by Stan and Gloria Cowley. The lodge was expanded and the tradition continues. For more information, call (403) 673-3622.

Lac Des Arcs and Grotto Mountain

surface.

At a small wooden platform you get a great view of the spring and the mud literally bubbling away as if it was boiling. Feel the water. It may not be warm enough to swim in, but it does stay above freezing throughout winter. This helps create a unique microclimate around the pond. Just beyond this point, keep your eyes open for the floral highlight of the trail—the bright colours of the yellow lady slipper.

Orchids

ORCHIDS ARE VERY primitive flowers, yet they are one of the most diverse, both in appearance and in the relationships they have with their pollinators. The yellow lady slipper is one of a large number of orchids found in Kananaskis Country. Other lady slipper types include the white sparrows-egg orchid and the calypso orchid. These both have a large lip-like lower petal, which makes bees force their way in to collect nectar. This results in their collecting a rather large amount of pollen, which is transferred to the next orchid they land on, fertilizing it.

Another orchid, the northern green bog orchid, has selected an unlikely pollinator—mosquitoes. Male mosquitoes spend their lives collecting nectar. This plant has evolved to take advantage of this so when they come for their nectar, they also pick up some pollen as well. Without mosquitoes, we may not have this orchid. Maybe there is a reason for everything.

Other orchids found in Kananaskis include the blunt-leafed orchid, round-leafed orchid, striped coral root, and spotted coral root.

Yellow lady slipper

119

9. Sibbald Creek Trail

Mount Baldy from Sibbald Creek Trail

Just 8 km (4.8 mi.) south of the Trans Canada Highway, the 36-km (21.6-mi.) Sibbald Creek Trail (Highway 68) provides access to a quiet foothills valley with numerous exploration opportunities. Andrew Sibbald settled near Morley in 1875. His son Frank settled along Sibbald Creek 15 years later, and introduced cattle to the area.

The rolling country along this road owes much of its character to the huge glacier that flowed up the Bow Valley to the north. Although this valley seems separate from the Bow Valley, things were quite different at the peak of the ice age. As the Bow Valley Glacier left the mountains and suddenly found itself unrestricted by the valley walls, it began to spread out. This piedmont glacier, as this squat river of ice is known, literally spread right over the surrounding hills and spilled into this valley. Since the ice came from the northwest, features in the valley caused by the moving ice are oriented in that direction. As the ice melted, huge lakes formed in front of the shrinking glaciers. This major advance ended approximately 40,000 years ago. Subsequent advances were more limited in extent, and did not supply enough ice to spill over to the Sibbald area, leaving the valley ice-free. This freedom from ice led to its use as a travel corridor, and the earliest example of Fluted Point projectiles in western Canada were found there. Fastened to the tips of lances, they were a primitive, yet effective, hunting tool.

Highway 68

Highway 68 follows the route of Sibbald Creek and the Jumpingpound River. From its western entrance to the north of Mount Baldy, it climbs over the small divide between the Stoney Creek and Sibbald Creek drainages. From here it follows Sibbald Creek as it becomes a tributary of the Jumpingpound Creek. Eventually, it abandons the river to head north to its junction with the Trans Canada Highway (Highway 1). It meets Highway 1 just east of the Scott Lake Hill, the second-highest point on the Trans Canada Highway.

As the highway parallels

Opposite: Bald eagle

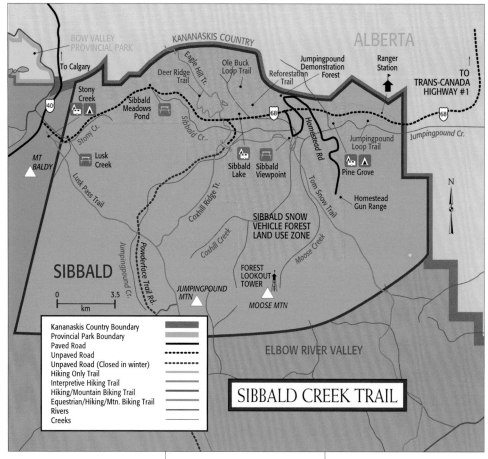

Legend:
- Kananaskis Country Boundary
- Provincial Park Boundary
- Paved Road
- Unpaved Road
- Unpaved Road (Closed in winter)
- Hiking Only Trail
- Interpretive Hiking Trail
- Hiking/Mountain Biking Trail
- Equestrian/Hiking/Mtn. Biking Trail
- Rivers
- Creeks

SIBBALD CREEK TRAIL

Sibbald Creek, it passes numerous sloughs and beaver ponds. These sloughs can be quite productive. Having shallow water, they warm up dramatically, and soft, muddy bottoms promote plant growth. Winter kill can be a problem for fish, as winter decomposition of plant material depletes the ponds of oxygen.

The channel of Jumpingpound Creek is considered a "misfit" stream. When it was originally carved, it was fed by incredible amounts of water as the mountain glaciers melted. Once the supply of ice was gone, a small river was left behind in a channel seemingly far too large for it.

Sibbald Lake

This tiny, shallow lake was formed when a large block of glacial ice was buried beneath a series of outwash deposits as the Bow Valley Glacier melted 40,000 years ago. When a block of ice is buried, it may remain as ice for a lengthy period before melting. As it melts, the material lying on top of it collapses into the hole left behind. This hole fills with the now-released water, and a lake results. Many of the small lakes at mountain fronts were formed in this way. Sibbald Lake is not very deep, only 2.1 m (7 ft.) at its deepest point. Some of its water supply today comes from underground springs, which helps keep the level consistent. Large glacial deposits adjacent to Bateman Creek nearby, reflect the deposit of glacial debris that originally held the pond-forming ice chunk.

The lake is popular with campers, but also with fishermen that like to test their luck in its placid waters. It's regularly stocked with rainbow trout. The day use area also serves as a trailhead for numerous hiking trails in the area, including Deer Ridge,

Jumpingpounds

The bison once ruled the plains

FOR GENERATIONS, the buffalo meant life to the Indians of the plains. Its meat was eaten and its skins kept them warm. Little was wasted, and the immense herds seemed like they would last forever. Before the introduction of the horse and the gun, a very creative method had to be devised to hunt these potentially dangerous beasts. For most of the prehistory of the plains, the method of choice was the jumpingpound. Since bison are a herd animal, the hunters needed to enlist the assistance of neighbouring family groups, and before long the annual buffalo hunt became an important social and religious event.

The bison were slowly gathered in areas known as collection basins. Rock cairns and man-made changes to the landscape help trace the route through which the bison were moved. To these early hunters it was critical that every bison die. They believed bison could talk, and if any survived, they would warn the others. That would end the chance of any future hunts on that cliff.

On the final day, dozens of hunters would line the route to the cliff. Some would cover themselves in animal hides and try to look inconspicuous. At the last minute, they would all jump up and whip the herd into a frenzy. The bison stampeded towards the cliff and their poor eyesight never warned them of their impending doom. By the time they saw the chasm, it was too late to stop, and they tumbled over the edge to their death. Jumping-pound Creek has numerous pound sites, though they are further downstream, where the banks are high and steep.

Another site south of Calgary is known as Head-Smashed-In Buffalo Jump. It is the most heavily studied of these hunting sites, and was used consistently for more than 5,000 years.

Eagle Hill, Ole Buck Loop, Sibbald Flat, and Reforestation Trail.

Sibbald Meadows Pond

This pleasant little pond is rarely without a fishermen or two, with fly rods a-flicking. It looks like it has always been part of the landscape, but it was artificially created in 1982. At that time, the Sibbald Creek floodplain was dredged, and the fill removed. This depression was supplemented with a partial dam to raise the water level even more. It covers 4.8 ha (12 acres) and has a maximum depth of 4.5 m (15 ft.). With the consistent water level created by the dam, the lake sees many families spending time along its shores. Small inflatable boats or family canoes find their way into its calm waters.

Powderface Trail

Winding south from the Sibbald Creek trail, this narrow, 36-km (21.6-mi.) gravel road provides excellent fair-weather access to the Elbow Valley. It climbs gradually to crest a small divide between the Jumpingpound and Canyon Creek drainages. It follows the dividing point between foothill and mountain. The jagged faces of the Fisher Range to the west contrast with the rolling foothills to the east. Along its length the road provides access to numerous trail systems, and is the only vehicle link between the Kananaskis and Elbow Valleys. It is recommended in fair weather only.

The road was built around 1952 to link the valleys of the Elbow and Jumpingpound rivers. During this period, the Eastern Rockies Forest Conservation Board was expanding facilities and improving roads, to ensure access in the case of forest fire. The Forestry Trunk Road was part of this same program of expansion.

Sibbald Trails

1. Jumpingpound Loop

If you're looking for a good early-season trail, Jumpingpound Loop may fit the bill. It receives lots of sun because of its south facing exposure, so it clears of snow earlier than many other trails. It also has a very moderate gradient, allowing the legs to work their way back into shape. There are numerous access points, but the Jumpingpound Ranger Station makes an easily located trailhead. The entire loop is 9 km (5.4 mi.) in length, but it can

be broken down into shorter lengths.

The trail crosses Highway 68 at the eastern and western ends. The portion to the north of the highway climbs from the Ranger Station and wanders along a low ridge that has some sunny slopes facing south. These explode with prairie crocus early in the season and are a favourite place for spotting these pleasant flowers. Moose Mountain looms to the south, standing high above the foothills.

The stretch south of the highway follows the channel of Jumpingpound Creek, crossing several small tributaries and providing a lovely walk.

2. Cox Hill

From the summit of Cox Hill, the foothills spread out at your feet. The mountains tower to the west, and logging activity in the area shows a patchwork pattern. In order to attain this lofty vantage, there is some elevation to be gained—700 m (2,310 ft.) of it. The trailhead is Dawson day use, just south of

Sibbald Creek Trail on Powderface Trail. The loop is 19.5 km (11.7 mi.) long, and begins climbing almost immediately.

The climb takes you through a mixed forest of aspen and lodgepole pine, along with some old growth of white spruce. Just when your gut senses the summit, you see a steep assault for the last kilometre. When you crest the top, take a look around. To the west you can see all the way to Mounts Sparrowhawk, Lougheed, and Kidd. To the north, the flat face of Mount Yamnuska stands defiantly above the plains.

After drinking in the fabulous view, hikers may wish to return the same route, but for bikers, all that pushing is now rewarded with a steep descent towards Jumpingpound Ridge trail. At kilometre 8.8 (mile 5.3) you can exit down the northern end of Jumpingpound Ridge trail, or continue on to ride this ridge as well.

3. Jumpingpound Ridge

This excellent ridge can be

Tom Lusk

LUSK CREEK and Lusk Pass take their names from one of the most colourful guides in the area. Tom Lusk was a hard-working, hard-drinking man. He was Martin Nordegg's guide when he prospected the coal seams on Mount Allan. Lusk was a tough Texan who arrived in the area around 1895 and quickly established a reputation as a man who could get the job done. He wore a big stetson and a red bandanna. Any who saw Tom in town may have assumed, as did Nordegg, that he

was a drunk. However, on the trail he never touched a drop. It was too difficult to justify the weight of all the liquor, and the bottles were too easily broken. But when the season was done, he'd retire to his cabin with several cases of whiskey. He would divide them up for the six winter months and never drink more than his ration. When the Stoneys saw the smoke stop billowing, they would stop in and either re-light his fire, or arrange a funeral.

Sunset along the Trans Canada Highway

done by hikers as a day trip or by mountain bikers as part of a combination of Cox Hill and this trail. It begins along Powderface Trail, 11 km (6.6 mi.) south of its junction with Highway 66.

The trail climbs steeply through deep forest cover for three kilometres. Cyclists will find this stretch a combination of pushing and riding. The trail is wide and has a good surface. From the junction with Cox Hill, stay on Jumpingpound Ridge Trail and follow this wonderful, sinuous ridge towards the summit of Jumpingpound Mountain. Although the trail doesn't crest the true summit, it is open country and the summit easily accessible.

The views are not as grand as from Cox Hill, but the skyline is still dramatically open. The various peaks of the Elbow Valley loom to the south,

and the jagged Fisher Range owns the western sky.

The trail descends down the Canyon Creek drainage at kilometre 11.3 (mile 6.8) and meets Powderface Trail Road at the 12-km (7.2-mi.) mark. An alternate exit is located at kilometre 6.6 (mile 4.0) where the summit trail is a steep drop off the ridge to join Powderface Trail at kilometre 9.1 (mile 5.5).

4. Eagle Hill

From Sibbald Lake day use area, Eagle Hill climbs the divide between the Jumpingpound and Bow River drainages. The 7-km (4.2-mi.) trail climbs 330 m (1,089 ft.) before providing a pleasant, if not spectacular, view of the Bow Valley to the west and the Sibbald area to the south.

The summit also marks the boundary between Kananaskis

Country and the Stoney Indian Reserve. A fence runs along the boundary and provides the limit to northerly travel on this route. The Stoney Reserve runs from the summit of Scott Lake Hill on the Trans Canada Highway west to the Kananaskis River. To the north it extends well beyond the Bow River and Highway 1A.

The Stoneys traditionally preferred the mountains to the plains. On the plains, the Blackfoot were far too aggressive for the generally peaceful Stoneys. With the coming of missionaries like Reverend Robert T. Rundle, and his successors, Reverends George and John McDougall, many Stoneys were converted to Christianity. Culturally, they are related to the eastern Sioux as well as the Assiniboine Indians.

10. The Elbow Falls Trail (Hwy. 66)

Elbow Peaks from Powderface Ridge

T he hamlet of Bragg Creek provides services for the Elbow Valley, as well as the surrounding ranching country. The area has seen many visitors over the years. Long before the white man entered the wilderness, the ancestors of today's native Indians were hunting the shores of the

Elbow River. Later, men like David Thompson ushered in the fur trade by living and learning from the Blackfoot nations, as well as their neighbours, the Sarcee, both residing in this area in the early 1800s.

Before long the missionaries made their way westward, setting up the first catholic mission in southern Alberta just north of Bragg Creek. Not far from today's Clem Gardner Bridge, it was called "Our Lady of Peace Mission." A lonely stone cairn marks the spot today. Not far from the mission was a trading post operated by Sam Livingston.

Whiskey traders moved in around 1869 and then the Northwest Mounted Police, the forerunners of today's Royal Canadian Mounted Police. With the stability of police presence, settlers were not far behind.

Bragg Creek takes its name from Albert Warren Bragg. He arrived in 1886 with his younger brother John and attempted to set up a cattle ranch in the area. He was less than successful, and left prior to the turn of the century to look for greener pastures. To his surprise, a survey crew attached his name to the creek, and later a town sprung up

around it.

Today, Bragg Creek boasts bustling shopping malls, with visitors flocking in during the weekend and almost as quickly disappearing. It forms a jumping-off point for explorations of the nearby Elbow Valley, and is quickly growing into a popular artisans community with its numerous galleries.

West Bragg Creek

Few visitors explore the ranching country in the foothills west of Bragg Creek. It supports a growing number of housing developments, as Calgarians continually look to

Opposite: View west from Nihahi Ridge

127

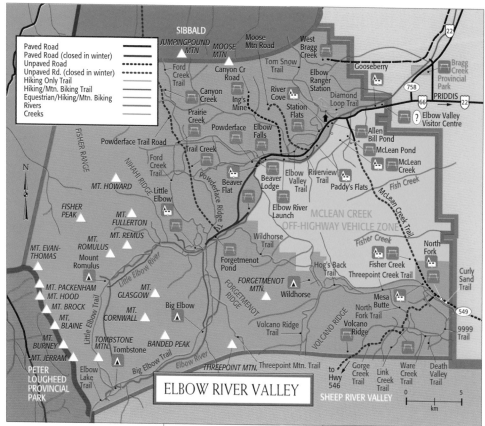

move out of the city. It provides a wonderful opportunity for country living within easy distance of Calgary. Slowly, the old ranches seem to be vanishing as more of these housing developments come on stream.

Not far from the town of Bragg Creek, Wintergreen ski hill provides a nice mix of moderate level skiing close to Calgary. Night skiing also makes this hill quite popular, as there is little in the way of night skiing opportunities farther into the mountains.

Farther west, where the west Bragg Creek road ends just within Kananaskis Country, a network of winter cross-country ski trails double as summer horseback and mountain-bike trails.

Ranching

It was not long after the arrival of the first cattle in southern Alberta in 1873 that ranching became a vital industry in the west.

By 1881 the local Indians had settled on reserves, the Mounties had brought stability to the area, and the railroads were moving westward, providing easy access to distant markets. Soon a flood of cattle moved into the area. The government allowed leases of up to 100,000 acres per man, spawning the large ranching operations of the early days. Most, like the

Quorn Ranch, were farther south, along the Sheep River. The Elbow was left to the independents, men like Sam Livingston and Albert Bragg.

During the summer, cattle would range far and wide. Each fall, representatives from area ranches got together for a roundup to bring the cattle in. The days were long, and the work hard, but as one pioneer rancher, Fred Ings, put it: "In looking back how I can see it! Hear it! Live it again! A roundup day! From the first call to roll out in the dawn till we stamped out the last coal of our fire and turned in, a little stiff and no-end weary, to sleep the dreamless sleep of youth."

Moose Mountain from the Trans Canada Highway

Highway 66—The Elbow Falls Trail

Travelling Highway 66 today, it's hard to believe the difficulties experienced by early travellers to this remote valley. Meandering west from Bragg Creek towards the Little Elbow Campground, its 100-km/hr (60-mi./hr.) speeds whisk visitors into the valley.

In the past, access was this valley's biggest challenge. With oil and gas wells appearing in the late 1920s, road quality was one of the major limitations to success.

The road was little more than a wagon trail beyond Bragg Creek. Heavy loads would sink in the mud. Trucks would unload at Bragg Creek and the gear was transferred to wagons for the bumpy ride down the valley. The early wells disappeared, but the

road lived on. In the 1950s, a gate was placed across the road near the present ranger station, and visitors were checked in by the local ranger. The rangers used pick and wheelbarrow to keep the road passable.

Upgrading during the 1980s brought a smooth surface to this formerly bumpy highway. As gravel was needed to resurface the road, it was taken from several large gravel pits adjacent to the highway. When the work was completed, the pits were flooded, and Allan Bill, McLean, and Forget-me-not ponds were formed. With the increased speed of traffic came the danger of hitting animals, particularly cattle, on the road. Drive slowly, and enjoy the view.

Moose Mountain

Over the years Moose Mountain has seen a lot of use. A.W. Bragg first settled along its lower slopes in 1886. Then it was mined for coal at the turn of the century. More recently it has been a fire lookout and a gas well site.

Dr. George Ings, also known for the Ings' Mine along Canyon Creek, was a Calgarian with a keen interest in coal. Beginning in the 1890s, he prospected the Bragg Creek area and discovered a seam of coal at the base of Moose Mountain. Unfortunately, despite a thousand tons of coal being taken out of this deposit, it never made it to market. Lack of proper transportation was the bane of many would-be mines.

Later, as forest fires became a concern, a lookout was

129

built on the rocky summit of Moose Mountain. Completed around 1929, it worked in conjunction with other lookouts to the south and north. Fires could quickly spread and threaten ranches downstream. Packhorses had to wind their way up a treacherous trail, where a single slip could mean tragedy, to the lookout site. Unlike most lookouts, the Moose Mountain site had its own spring for water.

After a truck road was built up to the summit in 1950, a new lookout was constructed beside the original. From its completion in 1952, until 1958, the old tower served as a

Entrance to the Canyon Creek Ice Caves

Rangers

THE FOREST RANGER is an enduring part of the history of the Rocky Mountains. As early as 1889 the Dominion Government began to worry about the impact of random logging on the health of forests. The Forestry Branch was organized, and rangers began to patrol what would later become southern Alberta. There were only two rangers for all of the southern part of this province, but they regulated cutting and kept an eye out for forest fires.

Dick Mackey was the district ranger in the Elbow Valley from 1952–60. As he put it:

"In those days when they wanted to hire a ranger, they wanted either some cowboy or logger or trapper; somebody who could live by himself, go back in the jungle by himself, look after himself, and, if you could read and write, so much the better."

Over the years the duties changed. As cattle moved into the valley, the ranger was placed

Park Rangers at a formal function

in charge of the rangeland. As coal mining and oil expansion increased, the forest rangers were kept busy regulating them. For many years the rangers controlled recreational access to the valley.

Until 1942 the rangers were laid off every fall. A seasoned ranger would arrange to be on the edge of his district by first snowfall. It would then take several weeks before he would re-

ceive his layoff notice.

The role of the ranger is still evolving. Today, the original duties of the forest ranger has been divided among several agencies. The Alberta Forestry Service still takes care of forest and resource concerns, but the Fish and Wildlife Department protects the area's wildlife, and Recreation and Parks facilitates recreation in the area.

source of firewood. Other towers, perched in locations too difficult to access by roads, were abandoned. In 1974, the lookout was again replaced, this time on its original 1929 foundation.

While the Alberta Forest Service struggles to ensure the Moose Mountain lookout station has sufficient propane each season, the tower sits on a "gold mine" of fuel—natural gas. The mountain's twin summits form a perfect geological storage system for gas. The first well, Moose Dome 1, was drilled in 1927, and a second, Moose Dome 2, in 1935.

Model Oil drilled a well in 1936, and McCall–Frontenac in 1941. Although these wells are no longer active, the mountain is still providing gas. Shell drilled their first well in 1960, right next to the McCall–Frontenac well. Unfortunately, with no compressor station or pipeline, the gas remained in the ground. Four other wells were drilled over the years, and finally, after a long public consultation process, Shell received approval to further develop the gas wells. In 1985 they opened the Moose Mountain Compressor Station, to which the

five wells were attached. The gas from the wells travels by pipeline to Esso's Quirk Creek gas plant, 28 km (17 mi.) south. It is processed there, and then it continues along the pipeline to help satisfy the growing demand for natural gas.

Canyon Creek

Canyon Creek has played an important part in the valley's history. One of the first wells, drilled by Moose Dome Oils, was drilled along the creek in 1927. Without transportation or pipelines, however, the gas stayed in the ground. What it

Wild Horses

BETWEEN THE VALLEYS of the Elbow and Sheep rivers, numerous bands of wild, or feral, horses roam. Descendants of formerly-domestic stock, their wild spirit can be seen in the fire in their eyes. It's hard to imagine horses as "wild," but the first time you set eyes on a feral band, their proud and wary nature quickly removes any doubts.

These stocky animals resemble a draft horse, with thick joints and heavy build. Their manes blow untamed in the breeze, and the mares are often accompanied by young colts. Although they add a touch of romance to the valley, they can be a real hazard to equestrian users. Wild studs are very aggressive in their attempt to increase their herd, and steal mares in season.

Bert Ostroski, a former Kananaskis employee and range rider, had one of his prize mares stolen by a "wildie." It took him two months to track her down, and after he finally recaptured

Wild horses still roam the foothills

her, he was rewarded with the birth of a half-wild filly. Make sure you avoid bringing mares in season into the area.

At certain times in the past, permits were available to capture wild horses. These animals were generally sold to meat-packing plants, but the lucky ones were trained and used as pack animals. The main areas for wild horses include the McLean Creek, Quirk Creek, Mesa Butte, Death Valley, and Muskeg Creek areas.

The numbers are small, but the lucky traveller may get to see them wandering their range.

They are very territorial, with the stud marking his territory with "stud piles." These manure heaps warn other studs to stay clear, unless they wish to challenge the resident stud. Today, the wild horses of Kananaskis have protected status, and are free to roam unmolested.

Elbow Falls

Whiskey Traders

IN 1869 THE Hudson's Bay Company relinquished its claim on Canada's vast western lands. With their departure the west was left devoid of Government representation. Whiskey traders from the United States flooded north into Canadian territory, to sell "rot-gut" to the Indians in exchange for furs. Lacking the long-term perspective of the Hudson's Bay Company, they had no interest in the well-being of the natives with whom they traded, and in short order, whiskey destroyed many villages.

Jean L'Heureux, a self-appointed missionary, wrote the Dominion Government begging for assistance. In his letter describing a two-year period at one post, he stated:

"Twelve thousand gallons of liquor were sold to Indi-
ans…Without counting the more than six hundred ounces of strychnine distributed to the Indians, more than one hundred and twelve persons have perished in these orgies and horrors."

Several posts were opened in the Elbow Valley area. The most notorious was operated by Fred Kanouse. He arrived on the banks of the Elbow in 1871 and built a three-room log post. The Indians traded by way of a long tunnel with a trap door. If a customer got out of hand and tried to break in, the trap could be released.

After an argument with one customer, Kanouse was wounded. In retaliation he killed the battle chief, White Eagle. The resulting battle lasted three days. Rein-
forcements arrived on day four, and the fort was saved for the time being.

Kanouse returned for one more season of trading, and described it as "quite successful." That same year, trader Dick Berry set up a post 20 km (12 mi.) upstream from Kanouse, but he was ambushed and killed by one of his customers.

In the fall of 1874, the Northwest Mounted Police arrived on the prairies, and brought an end to the whiskey trade. Crowfoot, the famous Blackfoot Chief, stated: "If the police had not come to this country, where would we all be now? Bad men and whiskey were killing us so fast that very few of us indeed would have been left today. The police have protected us as the feathers of a bird protect it in winter."

did accomplish for the area was a road, allowing access to this pleasant valley and opening it up for future development.

Natural gas started the ball rolling and it still plays a vital role along this roadway. Today, Shell operates a compressor station adjacent to the road. Since 1985 the compressor station has piped their gas 28 km (16.8 mi.) to a processing plant at Quirk Creek. Here it is processed to separate the sweet gas from the liquids and to remove the sulphur content. Following processing, the gas follows pipelines to Edmonton, and on to various other markets. From the end of the main road, a gated access road provides Shell with the ability to service some of its well sites.

Adjacent to the Canyon Creek Roads junction with Hwy. 66 is the Elbow River launch, which provides paddlers easy access to the river.

Ice Caves

Caves are not uncommon in the Rockies. Limestone, one of the predominant rocks of the mountains, is easily dissolved. The Canyon Creek ice caves were discovered in 1905 by Stan Fullerton. They are dark, damp, and full of ice. In the 1970s, more careful studies were undertaken, revealing 494 m (1,630 ft.) of tunnels. In 1983 four different caverns, located well inside the mountain face, were accessible. In subsequent years, variations in weather caused the entrances to seal with ice, making all but the main cave entrance impassable. Due to the potential dangers of caving, it is not recommended that novices attempt to penetrate beyond the main cavern.

Elbow Falls

The waters of the Elbow River plunge over a hard outcrop to form one of the highlights along Highway 66. It is the largest waterfall in Kananaskis Country, and one of the most popular stopping points along the valley.

Even at the turn of the century, people travelled long distances to see the falls. One such visitor was Monica Hopkins, who travelled for 2.5 days and reached the falls in 1910. She wrote in a letter: "The Falls are beautiful, not very large or high, but above them the river comes down in rapids, and the background of snow tipped mountains with dark tinges on the sides, and nearer the river the poplars in all the beauty of their autumnal colouring was a perfect picture."

Today, the falls still conjure up the same feelings. In keeping with Kananaskis' mandate to provide access for all users, the falls site was renovated around 1984 to make the trail wheelchair accessible. It also added railings to discourage climbing near the cliff edge. Some silly souls have jumped from the rocks into the deep pool beneath the falls—a very dangerous game. Park rangers

North America's First Hostel

Raising the tent wall at the first Bragg Creek Hostel

ALSO IN west Bragg Creek was the first Youth Hostel in North America. It was spearheaded by Mary and Catherine Barclay, who tried to sell the idea to just about anyone who crossed their paths. Converts included Ida and Harry White, who rented them the land for their first venture. On July 1, 1933, they set up a 12 ft. x 14 ft. tent, with cupboards made of apple boxes, a grass floor, and a primitive toilet.

In 1936, the hostel was moved to a site donated by Tom Fullerton. The hostel building was later replaced, only to burn down in 1984. That fire marked the end of hostelling in Bragg Creek, but hostels still remain popular elsewhere. The Ribbon Creek Hostel is now Kananaskis Country's sole hostel. To Mary Barclay, hostelling was "A right idea that once seen could never be destroyed!"

View from Moose Mountain Road

have had to install a permanent rescue cable beneath the rock face to facilitate the rescue of some of these swimmers. There are dangerous undercurrents beneath the foam. Please don't go beyond the railings.

Rainy Summit

The forests within the Bow corridor would burn, if left alone, about every 80 years. In 1981, this site had a 110-ha (275-acre) fire, which was followed by a salvage cut, meaning commercially salvageable timber was removed. To these forests, fire is an essential force, a process of renewal, and is required for life by many fire-adapted species. Some, like the lodgepole pine, rarely reproduce in the absence of fire. Its cones are tightly sealed with a hard wax and generally will not open until the wax is melted by the heat of a fire.

Poplars and aspens send

Mule Deer

out horizontal roots just below the surface that will, in turn, periodically send up a new shoot. When a fire moves through the stand, the trees are killed, but the root system will often survive. Before you know it, suckers start appearing and a new stand begins.

For local animals, when the fire burns itself out there's an abundance of exposed seeds.

Grouse and squirrels take advantage of these easy pickins', and those they miss quickly sprout in the carbon-rich soils. Soon new trees and shrubs are replacing the blackened stumps, and a whole new generation has begun.

Deer and elk wander the margins and take advantage of a healthy food supply as new growth takes over the burn.

The foothills from Nihahi Ridge Trail

Studies show that many shrubs important to grizzlies are more prevalent on burn sites when compared to old growth. The same study found that increasing fire suppression since the 1920s has led to the encroachment of conifers into shrub fields, leaving less food for the bears and, in the long run, fewer bears.

Cobble Flats

This pleasant day use area, located along the shores of the Elbow River, is a quiet, remote site for a picnic. It lies beneath the slopes of Forget-me-not Mountain, and links up with the Mount Quirk Exploration Road on the other side of the river. In the early 1990s, Shell drilled a well on Mount Quirk. During this time, a bridge provided easy access to this area, but as the well turned out to be a dry hole, the bridge was removed and the access closed.

Powderface Trail

In the shadow of Nihahi Ridge, Powderface Trail trends northward towards the Sibbald Creek Trail. Captain John Palliser passed this way in 1858 while doing the first surveys of the area. The name of the road and the surrounding ridge honours Tom Powderface, a Stoney Indian who lived in the Bragg Creek area.

Signs indicate that it is not recommended for travel, but in good weather it is a wonderful alternate route, providing access to Sibbald Creek Trail and Highway 40. It is the only alternate to backtracking along Highway 66, and is worth the adventure.

As it winds its way north, Powderface Trail passes beneath the convoluted slopes of Compression Ridge, and Mount Bryant to the west. To the east, the slopes of Powderface and Jumpingpound Ridges, as well as Cox Hill,

have a rolling appearance. The route is important, as the road follows the juncture of foothill and mountain. To the west, Nihahi Ridge, named for the Stoney Indian word for "rock," forms the official start of the Front Ranges of the Rocky Mountains.

Because of Kananaskis Country's multiple-use mandate, numerous logging projects have been undertaken along this road. The logging traffic means that it will require some extra caution to traverse this narrow road.

End of the Line

At the western end of the valley, Highway 66 is blocked by a solid wall of mountains. Suddenly the rolling foothills give way to the jagged peaks of the Rockies. Highway 66 meets Powderface Trail and the road crosses Ford Creek and ends in a campground. Henry Ford (1866–1933) was a rancher in

the Priddis area near the turn of the century. For many years this site used his name. The name "Little Elbow" recognizes the water source flowing to the south of the campground.

Although the mountain faces stop traffic today, they did not always do so. In past years 4x4 routes followed the rocky shores of the Little Elbow River, providing easy access to the backcountry. The route continued south to the Sheep Valley and made it possible to drive from one valley to the other. Today, the route is only used as a backcountry trail.

Elbow Valley Trails

1. Moose Mountain Ridge Road

Moose Mountain fire road takes you to the summit of Alberta's highest fire lookout and provides a 360° panorama. The 7-km (4.2-mi.) trail can be covered either as a hike, or as a combination of a 5.6 km (3.4-mi.) mountain-bike ride, followed by 1.4 km (0.8 mi.) of hiking on the final switchbacks to the summit.

The trail begins 7.5 km (4.5 mi.) along the Moose Mountain Ridge Road, which allows you to cover much of the elevation gain in your vehicle. However, there is still 914 m (3,016 ft.) left for you. Lookouts have been located here since about 1929, but this structure was built in 1974. When you reach the building, please don't approach it, as it is not a public facility. It is a residence and, as such, hikers are asked to respect the privacy of the tower staff.

To the east, views open up all the way to Calgary, whereas the western skyline is dominated by the transition from foothill to mountain. To the south stands another former lookout site, Forget-me-not Ridge.

2. Paddy's Flat Interpretive Trail

Radiating out from the various loops of the campground of the same name, this 2.2-km (1.3-mi.), self-guided interpretive trail is one of the most pleasant in the area. This campground, as well as this trail, shows the terraced nature of the Elbow Valley. The river valley contains thick layers of material deposited by meltwaters of the receding Elbow Valley glacier. As water levels fluctuated, the river cut into the material to varying depths. This created the terrace that this trail follows. Along the upper portion of the trail, through a pleasant aspen forest, watch for western wood lilies in June, as they are common near the turnaround point, where the trail drops down to the river. Along the river, a small sandy beach has formed where the river has created a small, shallow pool.

Ings' Mine

Dr. Ings at one of his claims

DR. GEORGE INGS was a Calgarian who had a keen interest in geology, particularly coal and oil geology. Beginning in the 1890s, he often rode through the foothills looking for potential deposits. His first venture near Bragg Creek was a failure due to a lack of transportation. In 1914 he discovered another coal seam, just as Bragg Creek's first oil well began drilling. He hired Bob Parker to operate the mine, and the coal supplied the Mowbray–Berkley oil well with fuel. The mine site was only accessible during the summer, due to the rugged nature of the road, but despite this, several thousand tons of coal were transported to the Bragg Creek well site.

Opposite: Tombstone Lake

Mount Romulus

From here, the trail follows the Elbow through numerous wildflower habitats, covering the spectrum from dry gravel washes to wet marshy areas. Each supports a different wildflower population, and in the moist areas watch for sparrow-egg orchids during June.

3. Powderface Ridge Trail

Beginning in a dark lodgepole pine forest, this trail climbs steadily to the summit at kilometre 5.5 (mile 3.3). The easiest place to begin the trail is at the junction of Highway 66 and Powderface Trail Road. Just beyond the cattle guard you'll see the trail heading up to the right side of this gravel road.

The climbing is unrelenting. Over the next 2 km (1 mi.) the trail climbs approximately 425 m (1,403 ft.) before reaching a grassy outlier. From here the trail stays in the open for a short distance, and the open slopes provide wonderful options for a sunny picnic. Generally the true summit, although dramatic, is far too

Powderface Creek Trail summit

windblown for lengthy relaxation.

From this point the climbing tapers off a little for the final push to the true summit. As you crest the peak, be prepared for the wind to hit you. From this point, the three main peaks of the Elbow Valley—Banded, Cornwall, and Glasgow—form the focal point to the southwest. Westward, the official start of the Rockies is marked by the knife-like Nihahi Ridge. To the east, watch the gradual shrinking of the foothills in the distance. Once you've enjoyed the view, you can either return back the

same route, or continue to a descent down Powderface Creek, slightly to the north of the summit.

4. Nihahi Ridge Trail

"Nihahi" is a Stoney Indian word meaning "rock." Appropriately, the trail climbs from the Little Elbow Campground towards the official start of the Front Ranges of the Rocky Mountains. Three kilometres from the campground to the trails end, it begins by following the Little Elbow Trail for 0.5 km (0.3 mi.) before branching off to the right towards the Ridge.

As it climbs, the trail rises

Mount Remus

over a broad knoll along the lower slopes, and then makes a final push to the end of the formal trail. From here, sitting on the boundary between mountain and foothill, the difference between them seems dramatic. The rolling hills to the east contrast sharply with the jagged, exposed slopes to the south and west.

Hawks and eagles may be seen soaring above the ridge. It may be work for humans to reach the ridge, but for the area's birds of prey, it's a simple flight.

5. Nihahi Creek

This wonderful trail is best left to the latter part of the season, when Nihahi Creek is largely devoid of water. Why? Because the trail follows the actual channel of this intricately carved canyon.

Beginning at the Little Elbow Campground, follow the Little Elbow Trail for 3.5 km (2.2 mi.) Take a fork to the right just before Nihahi Creek, and follow the trail as it climbs through the forest for 2.4 km (1.4 mi.) As it approaches the river canyon, it becomes clear

that it would be enjoyable to wander the river channel itself.

Early in the season, runoff flows in this channel, and it's difficult to explore without getting wet feet. Later, however, you can crawl around on polished limestone. The channel twists and bends, dropping like a waterslide towards the Little Elbow River.

As you reach the lower parts of the river, the channel widens out and becomes a boulder-strewn dry channel. Don't immediately abandon it for the trail in the woods, however. Interesting fossils may be seen in some of the large rocks strewn within the dry bed.

6. Elbow Loop

This long, wild loop takes you towards the headwaters of the Elbow River, in a circuit around the Big Elbow and Little Elbow rivers. The trip is 43.6 km (26.2 mi.) along a former fire access road and wide single-track trail.

From the Little Elbow Campground, cross the bridge over the Little Elbow and follow the Big Elbow River south between the round face of For-

get-me-not Ridge and the glacier-scarred face of Mount Glasgow. The wide track is easy to follow, and passes the Big Elbow Campground at kilometre 8.9 (mile 5.3). Beyond this rustic campsite it begins trending west, between Banded Peak to the north and Cougar Mountain to the south. For mountain bikers the next 7 km (4.2 mi.) has some technical obstacles, so caution is the watchword. As the trail approaches Tombstone Campground at 19.4 km (11.6 mi.), turn right and prepare for the uphill slog towards the headwaters of the South Fork of the Little Elbow. At the pass, at 23 km (3.8 mi.) and 2,280 m (7,524 ft.), the sheer slopes of Tombstone Mountain are dotted with alpine larch along the lower face. The drop off the pass, towards Mount Romulus Campground, is fast and rocky. From here the trail follows the Little Elbow as it winds its way back to the Little Elbow Campground at 43.6 km (26.2 mi.).

Forget-Me-Not Ridge over the Elbow River

7. Forget-Me-Not Rounder

Many of the longer routes in the Elbow Valley are designed to circumnavigate mountain ranges or peaks. This trail is no exception. It completely circles Forget-me-not Ridge, travelling 50.9 km (30.5 mi.) through rugged terrain that will entice the equestrian and challenge the mountain biker. It is not popular as a backpacking route, as some stretches lack the scenery so necessary to backpacking.

From the Little Elbow Campground, cross the Little Elbow River on its excellent bridge and follow the wide trail south for 4.3 km (2.6 mi.) where a nondescript trail branches off to the left. It's easy to miss, so watch for it. This is the beginning of Three-point Mountain Trail, and the start of the main climbing of the trip. Over the next 4.2 km (2.5 mi.), you'll climb from the river, at 1,591 m (5,250 ft.), to the highest point on the trail at 1,957 m (6,458 ft.) One of the

Sam Livingston

SAM LIVINGSTON was one of the pivotal settlers of this area. He had a knack for being at the right place at the right time. He arrived in the west during the 1860s, and settled near Fort Edmonton at a small post known as Fort Victoria. He and his wife Jane operated a trading business between Fort Garry (Winnipeg) and Edmonton. As the buffalo herds began to vanish in the early 1870s, the family began to look elsewhere. After all, Sam needed 700 buffalo pelts a year just to cover his costs.

They eventually settled near Our Lady of Peace Mission,

Sam Livingston

along the Elbow River. Here the buffalo were still plentiful. They even used the Livingston's cabin as a scratching post on occasion. During the summer of 1875 the Livingstons witnessed the end of an era. One morning, Sam watched a rider approach from a distance. He knew it was not an Indian by the way he sat in his saddle. It turned out to be one of the first mounted policemen to arrive on the plains. Soon thereafter the Livingstons packed up and moved to Fort Calgary, to become one of that community's first settlers.

Mountain biking provides endless views

Forget-me-nots

The delicate alpine forget-me-not

WHEN HIKING IN THE mountains, the alpine forget-me-not is one of the most pleasant flowers of the high country. Delicate, yet unmistakable, its sky blue petals and bright yellow centre are one of the rewards of climbing to the subalpine. Like most high altitude flowers, it is a perennial—there's just not enough time to grow from seed each year. They often stay very low to the ground, protected within, or beneath, a rock slope. When you encounter forget-me-nots, keep your eyes open for some of the other common alpine wildflowers.

best viewpoints on the route, you can see Banded Peak and Mounts Cornwall and Glasgow in the western sky, and Threepoint Mountain to the south.

This trail branches onto the wet Volcano Creek Trail and follows it to a junction with Volcano Ridge Trail at 19.7 km (11.8 mi.). After a short, steep climb, the Ridge trail is wide and smooth for most of its length. As the trail approaches the deep canyon of Threepoint Gorge, it's hard not to marvel at the power of nature to carve such a spectacle. Follow the signed junctions to Wildhorse Trail, and drop down to the river at kilometre 45.5 (mile 27.3). A ford of the frigid Elbow River brings you to Cobble Flats day use area. From here, a quick pavement spin returns you to the Little Elbow Campground at kilometre 50.9 (mile 30.5).

Lookout

A FIRE LOOKOUT was built in 1954 atop the slopes of Forget-me-not Ridge. This was part of a general expansion of forest-fire protection programs during this period. It was a tiny, 12 x 12-ft. cabin, but each summer, lookout personnel formed the front line against fire. In 1975 it was abandoned, and two years later the building was burned. Eventually even the access road was reclaimed, leaving little evidence of its presence. Why was it removed? It had become redundant—other lookouts covered its area. During its heyday, motorcycles enjoyed roaring up the road to the lookout, and this provided part of the impetus for the road being reclaimed.

11. Sheep Valley

The Sheep Valley explodes into golden fall colours

Turner Valley is the primary access point for the Sheep River Valley, and it is known for its pivotal role in the development of the oil industry in Alberta. But long before the rigs arrived, the ranchers took over the plains. Southern Alberta was settled much later than areas farther

north. Among the first large ranches were the O.H. (later the Rio Alta), established in 1879, and the Quorn Ranch, in 1884.

Not far behind the ranchers were prospectors, who moved into the foothills. Harry Denning Sr. opened a coal mine along the shores of the Sheep River in 1888. Today Denning is recognized as Turner Valley's first settler.

In 1887 Sam Howe and John Ware, took an empty whiskey bottle and filled it with oil they discovered in a slough. The site was right where Turner Valley is located today.

By 1891, with the influx of settlers on the rise, the need for timber brought the loggers. Donald Morrison began to run logs down the Sheep River for use in the railway under construction between Calgary and Fort MacLeod.

When Dingman No. 1 well came into production in May of 1914, an oil boom was set off. Over the years hundreds of oil companies have come and gone, but Turner Valley is still producing oil and gas today.

To access the Sheep River Valley, head west on Highway 546.

Highway 546

Winding through some of the province's premier ranching country, Highway 546 provides a pleasant introduction to the prosperity of the Sheep River valley .

The first road down this valley serviced the Lineham Logging Camp, and passed Harry Denning's coal mine. Cutting trees in the valley as early as 1891, they built the first rough road. Numerous other mines were attempted in the lower part of the valley, and in 1903 Pat Burns opened a coal mine farther up the valley, beyond the limits of the present road. The Burns com-

Opposite: Gibraltar Mountain

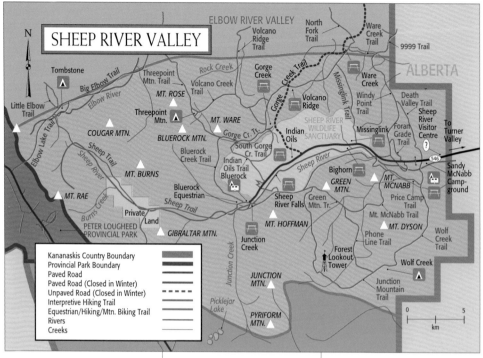

SHEEP RIVER VALLEY

pany had to build and maintain much of the road beyond Gorge Creek themselves. A planned railroad never materialized.

In 1948 surveying for a Forestry Trunk Road south to Coleman began. Four years later, in 1952, it was completed, along with numerous secondary roads designed to provide access to adjacent valleys. One route led from the upper Sheep past the Burns mine site and on to the Elbow Valley. With the naming of Kananaskis Country in 1977, this route was restricted to non-motorized traffic only.

Sheep River

The Sheep River was a vital waterway long before the first humans moved through its valley. From the early bands of nomadic hunters, to today's bands of nomadic hikers, it has formed the nucleus of this picturesque valley.

Although the river is responsible for carving this valley, glaciers had a dramatic impact on the landscape we see today. Numerous glaciers flowed down the valley of the Sheep, all converging near present-day Bluerock campground. At the height of glaciation the ice would have been approximately 275 m (908 ft.) thick at this point. As the glacier became less constricted by the narrow valleys of the upper Sheep, it spread out into several piedmont glaciers. As these glaciers melted, a 15-km-long (9-mi.-long) lake formed between Turner Valley and the eastern boundary of Kananaskis Country. It was short-lived, and quickly drained away as more ice melted to the east.

By 40,000 years ago the main Sheep River valley was free of ice. Later advances were limited to small cirque glaciers, which flowed only as far as Gorge Creek.

Sharing its Mount Rae headwaters with the Elbow River, the Sheep was the victim of stream "piracy." As the Elbow River extended its headwaters, runoff was diverted from the Sheep. Its many tributaries join the Sheep, and they combine to include more than 1,000 km (600 mi.) of channel.

The upper Sheep River follows the landscape, the mountain ramparts determining the route of its channel. East of Bluerock Campground the river cuts across the landscape to take on an eastern course.

Now its waters are diverted for irrigation. Its waves see the occasional whitewater paddler, and free-ranging cattle

Sticky purple geranium

still drink from it. It is as important today as it was when the first natives wandered this remote wilderness.

Sandy McNabb

Sandy McNabb recreation area is one of the focal points of the trip along the Sheep River. Its day use area provides wonderful picnic sites along the Sheep River. There is also an interpretive trail with panoramic views of the surrounding valley and some slopes covered with wildflowers.

The site has a terraced landscape, with numerous steps gradually dropping towards the river. These were formed as the river cut away at glacial deposits. The campground takes advantage of these levels and allows for a variety of views and camping options.

Sandy McNabb, after whom the site is named, was employed in the oilpatch during the 1920s and 1930s. He worked for companies like Dalhousie Oil and Imperial Oil. Royalite Oil developed an association with Imperial dur-

ing the depression. McNabb, lucky to have a job during trying times, worked on behalf of Royalite to provide food assistance to the oilfield workers. He would buy cows and, with the help of some of the men, butcher them and deliver the meat to the families he felt needed it most.

An avid camper, McNabb's favourite site was at the mouth of Coal Creek; it became known as "Sandy McNabbs Camp" as early as 1916. As the site became increasingly popular, the Alberta Forest Service began to provide simple facilities. It was upgraded again during the 1950s for camping, and improved road access brought more people into the valley.

McNabb was also an avid sportsman, and helped organize a hunt club in Turner Valley. Early every Thursday, two members would head out and lay a trail, and the hunt would commence in the evening. As more and more fences were put up, it became increasingly difficult to find a good site for hunting.

Sheep Ranger Station

The Sheep Ranger Station forms the headquarters for information on the Sheep River valley. Located just before you reach the Sandy McNabb recreation area, it can provide you with any information you require to make your time in the valley more enjoyable.

Alberta Recreation and Parks is responsible for, as its name implies, recreation. Over the years, they have taken over some of the early duties of the Alberta Forest Service, allowing that agency to focus on their area of expertise. Over the years, recreational use has increased, and now is the principle use of this valley. The oil wells and coal mines have disappeared, and logging is much more limited in extent. With the increasing demands of hikers, mountain bikers, horseback riders, hunters, and fishermen, the park's staff are kept busy.

This building is relatively new, and provides a new home for the park's staff. Previously, they based their operations within the Bighorn Sheep Sanctuary, as the Alberta Forest Service had done before them. This modern centre places them at the entrance to the valley, creating a higher profile and allowing them to keep better tabs on valley use.

R.B. Miller Station

With the natural potential for research in the sanctuary, the R.B. Miller Biological Station of the University of Alberta is well situated.

R. B. Miller was a biologist engaged in fish studies in the

Oil and Gas

Turner Valley, 1935

ALBERTA'S OIL BOOM began in the Turner Valley area. When Dingman No. 1 blew in during May of 1914, the whole character of this sleepy area changed. During one 24-hour period, more than 500 oil and gas companies were formed in Calgary.

The early drills were cable tool rigs, which worked by lifting and dropping heavy cutting tools repeatedly. This setup was so successful that they became known as "Canadian Rigs."

At the helm of Calgary Petroleum Products Company was A. W. Dingman and W. S. Herron. Their Dingman No. 1 well was the deepest well drilled at that time. The oil was a light naphtha, which was quite pure and could be burned in car engines without refining.

In 1924 another major strike, Royalite No. 4, brought renewed interest to the Turner Valley fields. Subsequent studies showed that most of the wells had been abandoned before being drilled deep enough. Most had struck gas, and further evaluation of drilling data showed that the gas was merely a cap over the larger oil reserves. Armed with this new knowledge, Royalite No. 4 drilled to a record depth of 1,949 m (6,395 ft.) in 1936, and became the area's first big producer of crude oil. Almost overnight, towns like Turner Valley and Black Diamond doubled in size. Other tiny communities grew from the plains with names like "Little Chicago," and "Little New York." The latter survives today under the more fitting moniker of Longview.

In 1949 oil was discovered in Leduc, near Edmonton, and the importance of Turner Valley quickly declined. Many of the wells are still producing, among them the Quirk Creek gas field developed in the 1960s. Owned by Imperial Oil, the gas is processed at the Quirk Creek Gas Plant and then moved to market through a series of pipelines.

In 1929 the Indian Oils Company started drilling in the Sheep Valley, but abandoned the effort the same year.

Hell's Half Acre

The early wells wasted much of the natural gas produced, as there was little market for it at that time. Pipelines to Calgary had yet to be built, so there was little means to move the gas to market. Some was used to heat the bunkhouses and local homes, and most of the remainder was burned in countless flare stacks around Royalite No. 4. The gas production during the peak, in excess of 5.7 million m^3 (200 million ft.^{3}) daily, was enough to have heated New York City. The combination of strong skunk-like odour and flames led to the area's nickname— "Hell's Half Acre."

Goddy McRae of Turner Valley, in the book "In The Light of the Flares", recalled: "The view was breathtaking! A great fairyland was before us...The brightness of the light and the intensity of the heat were frightening at first. Only those, who have stood as we did, understand. We turned northward to see Hell's Half Acre, where a gigantic flame played in the embankment. We stood and marveled at the strange light and the deafening roar."

Sheep Sanctuary

THE SHEEP RIVER WILDLIFE SANCTUARY was first established in 1973 to protect critical bighorn sheep winter range. This is increasingly essential, especially with improved access to the valley over the past few years. This, coupled with hunting pressures adjacent to the sanctuary and numerous grazing allotments overlapping its boundaries, is putting the squeeze on the area's sheep population.

Bighorn sheep are an animal unique to high places. Female sheep are often mistaken for mountain goats, due to their short goat-like horns. However, goats are snow-white in colour and have black horns. The females, or ewes, spend the summer at low elevations with the lambs, while the rams prefer to stay in bachelor herds higher up the mountains. In late fall they congregate for the rut on the wide flats near the research centre. The sound of two rams butting heads echoes like a gunshot, and carries for

miles on the wind. The successful male wins the right to mate with the harem. The rut leaves him in a weakened condition just before the long winter. This can have fatal consequences if sufficient reserves to survive this difficult season are lacking.

The diet of bighorn sheep includes grasses, flowers, and other foliage. During winter, they climb towards high ridges, where ever-present winds keep the grasses exposed. Occasionally they become part of the diet of predators, primarily cougars and wolves.

With the large resident sheep population, the sanctuary is an ideal place for research. Studies focus on diseases (lungworm), die-offs, grazing conflicts, and overpopulation. As part of the study, the sheep are ear-tagged, and some are radio-collared.

The sanctuary has also been the site of a number of reintroduction programs. Although the Sheep District of Kananaskis includes parts of four different registered traplines, fishers were trapped in northern Alberta and transplanted to the Sanctuary. During the same period, peregrine falcons were also reintroduced. Neither program was successful, and both animals are rare within the valley.

The Sheep River valley was also the home of a cougar study. The study took place in the early 1980s and dogs were used to track cougars, which were in turn tranquilized and radio-collared. Over a four-year period 28 different cougars were collared. As of 1985, estimates suggested that approximately six to eight females and two to three males were in the area.

Bighorn Sheep

area during the 1950s. He founded the Alberta Biological Station in 1950. Over the next seven years it expanded in size and scope. When Miller died in 1959 it was renamed the R. B. Miller Biological Station. During the summer months, students do research on everything from ground squirrels to grouse. The findings are regularly published in scientific publications and theses.

At various points in the valley, tall poles topped with chairs are visible. These are used as part of ground squirrel studies. The birds-eye view allows researchers to better study a colony of animals. They are one of the visible signs of ongoing research in the area.

Gorge Creek Trail Junction

This winding secondary road provides fair-weather adventure as it climbs from the Sheep Trail to access McLean Creek Trail and, in turn, the Elbow Valley.

The road crosses over three divides, creating a roller coaster of steep driving. The first separates Gorge Creek from Ware Creek. It is followed by a second divide to join Link Creek, and concludes with a serious climb towards Threepoint Creek. This final stretch ascends more than 200 m (660 ft.) in just over 4 km (2.4 mi.) before dropping almost as rapidly to join the McLean Creek Trail.

The road was built along an old pack trail to link up with the Elbow Valley during the Eastern Rockies Forest Conservation Board tenure. They undertook extensive improvements to road access to facilitate watershed and forest fire protection. Good roads meant that fire crews could rapidly attack fires in remote areas.

During upgrading of this route during the late 1970s and early 1980s, archaeological studies uncovered a long-lived and diverse culture. Finds showed a steady occupation from approximately 3,500 BC to 1,000 AD. Some of the artifacts included tools, made of both local and distant materials. This indicates that these early residents had extensive trading networks extending to the east and south.

Coal Mining

This valley contains a lot of coal, but its rugged landscape and limited road access, has repeatedly thwarted attempts to commercially mine the resource.

Early settlers occasionally dug some coal for their own use, but the amount was small. The first commercial coal mine was undertaken by Harry Denning Sr. in 1888. His mine was located west of the town of Turner Valley, and the excellent quality of the coal led to further interest in the reserves. Names like Coal Creek

Threepoint Gorge

and Indian Oils reflect this early period of exploration.

George Austin, a Dominion Land surveyor, surveyed many of the early coal leases. In 1906, Government reports list two mines in operation–Denning's and another along Coal Creek. Many claims were filed along the creek due to its rich deposits, but few were developed. Coal Creek mine, near present-day Sandy McNabb Campground, was opened in 1915 by Dave Blacklock. To get the coal out, Blacklock waited until winter when a sled could be dragged over the frozen river.

Frank Swanson opened the Windy Point Coal Mine about 1918. Slightly west of the present day Ranger Station, the coal was of poor quality, almost as soft as peat, and pro-

A quiet moment at Sheep Falls

vided little heat. Despite this, the site was worked again between 1920 and 1931.

The Indian Oils Company operated a mine from 1929–31. It was situated near the present Indian Oils day use area. The site was reopened in 1940, and the tunnel mined until 1945. Then a strip mine opened on the site, which was worked until 1951.

The only mine with any staying power was the Burns Mine. Registered in 1903, the company acquired mining rights to 85 quarter-sections along the upper Sheep River Valley. The mine site remained in private hands, even after the Forest Reserves Act of 1906 and 1911 restricted private ownership within the reserves. It still remains as the only private land in the valley.

Prospector Julius Rickert discovered coal along the upper Sheep River at the turn of the century. He managed to interest Pat Burns in the site, and was assigned a one-twentieth interest in the holdings. The mine was doomed from the start. Although three mines were opened, one strip mine and two tunnel mines, transportation remained the major difficulty. The coal had to be taken out along a rough road. The Burns Company built and maintained the road beyond Gorge Creek, while the Forestry Department kept the rough cart track passable to the east of the creek. For years, Burns pushed to have a railway built to the minesite, and in 1918, the Calgary and Southern Railway was incorporated to do just that. Although much of the right-of-way was cleared over the years, not a single track was ever laid. The fortunes of coal were falling and the oil industry was beginning to boom. The mine ceased operation in 1923, but in 1944, Allied Industrial Ltd. tried to reopen the site. In 1948 another attempt was made by eastern promoters. Neither was able to create a viable enterprise. Finally, in the early 1960s the mine was sealed for the last time.

When Kananaskis Country was named, mining was prohibited within its boundaries.

Sheep Falls

From the Indian Oils day use area, a short walk takes the visitor to Sheep Falls. The river and falls were known to the early native travellers of this valley as the "itou-kai-you." This name was used on David Thompson's first map of the area, and was later translated to "Sheep."

The falls has also been known as Shepherd Falls. Several documents relating to the Indian Oils coal mine refer to it by this name. The origin is unknown.

The falls is not large, but the water tumbles over the rock outcrop with a low rumble. It is created by a resistant layer of rock overlying softer shales. The shales are easily eroded, whereas the harder rock (sandstone or limestone) remains. As the soft rocks beneath the falls are removed, an overhang of hard rocks is created. In time, the weight of the water snaps off the overhang, and the falls moves slightly upstream.

Logging

Like most of the Kananaskis, the Sheep River valley has been extensively logged. Settlers arrived on the scene and the valley quickly fell under the axe. In the late 1880s, the Lineham Lumber Company began cutting along the Sheep and Highwood rivers. Crews

cut during the winter months and the logs were floated down the river during the spring flood.

By 1912 most of the valley's marketable timber had been cut. Large fires over the years took care of much of the remaining timber. Salvage cutting was the name of the game for much of the 20th century. The Bluerock Creek area was logged in 1947 by Napp Lefavre, but he was allowed to remove green timber as well as burned wood. Anything less than 25 cm (10 in.) in diameter had to be left untouched.

About the same time, the

Price Logging Camp operated along March Creek. Near the camp, a falls on Dyson Creek found a unique use. The foreman apparently used the falls as a walk-in "cooler" by storing fresh meat in a small cave hidden behind the waterfall.

Bluerock

The western extent of Highway 546 is marked by Bluerock Campground. However, prior to Kananaskis Country's official designation, four-wheel-drive vehicles regularly continued all the way to the Elbow Valley. The campground takes its name from Bluerock Moun-

Ranching's Golden Era

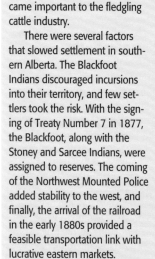

CATTLE ARRIVED IN southern Alberta in 1872, and it wasn't long before the Sheep River valley became important to the fledgling cattle industry.

There were several factors that slowed settlement in southern Alberta. The Blackfoot Indians discouraged incursions into their territory, and few settlers took the risk. With the signing of Treaty Number 7 in 1877, the Blackfoot, along with the Stoney and Sarcee Indians, were assigned to reserves. The coming of the Northwest Mounted Police added stability to the west, and finally, the arrival of the railroad in the early 1880s provided a feasible transportation link with lucrative eastern markets.

The first ranches were huge, some as large as 40,000 ha (100,000 acres). In 1881 the government introduced a land lease policy that allowed 21-year leases and a maximum of 40,000 ha. The cost was a tiny one cent per acre. Before long,

Rolling ranchland along Highway 546

wealthy investors opened ranches like the Quorn and the O. H. (later the Rio Alta). The growth was rapid. In 1880 there were only five ranchers with herds outside the Fort MacLeod market. By 1882 there were as many as 75 such operations.

Most of these ranches were British owned; though the image

is of the American-style cowboy, the true picture also included polo, horse racing, cricket, and tennis.

The large ranches tried to limit the influx of smaller operations. The Quorn in particular often used force. When Harry Denning opened his coal mine along the Sheep River, the tain, and has facilities for equestrian as well as traditional users.

The junction of Bluerock Creek and the Sheep River marks the official start of the Front Ranges of the Rocky Mountains. To the west, the sheer face of Gibraltar Mountain is a tribute to the extensive glaciers that scoured it.

Forest Fires

Fires are a natural part of the mountain ecosystem. During this century numerous fires made their way down the Sheep Valley. In 1910 most of the valley was charred by a huge fire. The summer had been hot and dry, with less than 1 cm (0.4 in.) of rain. A crew working for the Lineham Logging Company lost control of their campfire while working on the other side of the Misty Range, and the flames quickly jumped over the divide and spilled down the Sheep Valley.

In 1919 a fire was started by workers clearing the right-of-way for the Burns Coal Mine. It burned out the Indian Oils mine, luckily defunct at the time, and continued down the length of the valley. Because of the large number of fires that year, cattle had been moved out of the reserve as a precautionary measure.

The years 1929, 1936, and 1940 saw more fires. Fred Nash was District Ranger during that period, and he worked relentlessly to preserve his forests. One reporter described Nash's dedication: "He came dashing up on horseback, his face black with smoke and grime and his horse played out. He dashed into the corral, unsaddled, threw his saddle on a fresh Mount and galloped off—back to the fire line."

Despite the dangers, wages

Quorn sent John Ware to warn him to either move on or risk being burned out. Denning informed Ware that he could also play with fire, and was subsequently left alone. Another family, led by Agrippa and Walter Vine, was burned out.

By the mid-1880s, the government had developed new policies designed to quickly settle the west. This created difficulties for the large operations. The west was parceled into numbered sections of land, all open to purchase. Fences began to appear all over the area, restricting the cattle of the large operations. The golden age of ranching lasted less than 20 years, and was followed by the age of settlement.

In the Sheep River Valley, although there were few settlers living in the reserve area, the cattle roamed freely. One settler, Harry Holness, homesteaded in the location of the Old Sheep Ranger Station, located within the present Sheep Sanctuary. In 1911, when the Bow/Crow Forest Reserve was established, he was evicted, and moved his holdings to Calgary.

Death Valley

The first ranchers descending upon the west were amazed at the wonderful Chinook winds that blew from the mountains. The winds always kept enough forage exposed for the wintering herds. The thought of putting up hay in preparation for winter was considered a waste of time and money. They could always depend on the Chinooks.

After the hard winter of 1886-87, some ranchers began to question this decision, but it was the winter of 1906-07, "the year of the blue snows," that really changed their minds. That winter, several hundred horses and cows were trapped in a small box canyon in the Sheep Valley. In the spring, the winds carried the smell of rotting flesh, and to this day that valley is known as "Death Valley." That very spring the ranches started putting up hay, and they've been doing it ever since.

John Ware

John Ware was one of Alberta's most famous black cowboys. Born into slavery in South Carolina, he headed to Texas after the Civil War to become a cattle hand. He made his way to Alberta in 1882, helping Tom Lynch drive cattle north. He later worked for the Quorn Ranch before filing his own homestead claim in 1885, at the junction of present day Threepoint and Ware creeks. His "9999" brand became famous. He left in 1902 and moved to the Red Deer River where, only two years later, he died when his horse fell on him. Canada lost its most celebrated early black rancher the same year Alberta became a province. In 1970 a memorial was erected on the site of his original homestead.

Dysan Falls

were kept low during the depression to discourage arson. Fire fighters were paid 15 cents per hour for long days and dangerous work.

The last fire of note burned 26 ha (65 acres) around Bluerock Creek in 1964. It was contained quickly by fire crews flown in by helicopter. The modern age had arrived, and fire roads built only 20 years earlier were suddenly obsolete. The Alberta Forest Service had made the final transition from horses to helicopters.

Sheep River Valley Trails

1. Junction Mountain Fire Lookout

The 14.2-km (8.5-mi.), one-way trail to the fire lookout tends to be a mountain bike or horseback route due to the extended distance and lack of camping facilities along the route. However, those that do travel to the summit of this 2,230-m (7,359-ft.) vantage point, will be rewarded with excellent views of the surrounding ranges.

The trail begins at Indian Oils trailhead, 17 km (10.2 mi.) west of the Sheep River Information Centre. It drops down to the river, crosses a good-quality bridge, veers left, and travels through some stretches that stay wet because they are churned up by free-ranging cattle. The trail intersects Dysan Creek at kilometre 4.3 (mile 2.6) requiring a ford of this narrow, but cold, stream. Shortly after the ford, a final turn to the right onto the Junction Mountain Lookout Trail takes you to the summit.

The climbing is steady and steep for the entire route. When you approach the summit, the work suddenly feels worthwhile. To the west, the solid wall of Junction Mountain oversees the junction of the two branches of the Sheep River and provides an imposing sight. To the east, the foothills roll off into the distant plains. While here, please avoid the temptation to approach the lookout building.

2. Sandy McNabb Interpretive Trail

When Sandy McNabb first headed up the valley of the Sheep River, he had the choice of locating his campsite anywhere he wanted. He chose this bench above the Sheep River. His location is as appropriate today as it was then. This short, 1.8-km (1.1-mi.) interpretive trail takes you through the open forest of the campground and past a wonderful rest spot over the river.

As the trail opens up above the river, the grassy slope explodes into colour during early June. The three-flowered avens, along with the shooting star, sticky purple geranium, and western wood lily, all make an appearance. Its difficult to hike this trail during flower season and not spend a few minutes admiring these colourful characters.

View from Sandy McNabb Interpretive Trail

At the viewpoint a bench provides a place to take a load off and admire the river as it passes beneath your feet. Keep your eyes open for kayakers testing their luck in the currents.

The rolling character of the lower Sheep River Valley is evident in the views of the surrounding area. The river has its headwaters on Mount Rae, the same mountain that spawns the Elbow River to the north.

3. Sheep Trail

Beginning at Bluerock Campground, this watershed trail follows the Sheep River west and then north, towards its headwaters at the base of Mount Rae. It is as popular with horseback riders as it is with mountain bikers. Backpackers also like to travel its length to access numerous backcountry possibilities.

The trail follows the route of an old fire-access road joining the Elbow and Sheep river

valleys. Now closed to vehicle traffic, it passes an old coal mine at 12.3 km (7.4 mi.). The Burns Coal Mine operated on this site from 1903 to 1923. It was worked briefly again in 1944, but this venture failed. Near the mine site a trail branching to the south heads up Mist Creek (see next trail description). Beyond the junction, the trail begins trending northwest beneath the Misty Range, and towards the headwaters on Mount Rae. The trail finally joins the Elbow Pass Trail at the 22-km (13.2-mi.) mark. From this point, trails radiate towards all four compass points, providing numerous options for exploring.

4. Mist Creek

From the junction with Sheep Trail, the route along Mist Creek requires a lot of work before Mist Creek is ever reached. Between Storm Mountain and Gibraltar Mountain a glacier cut a low pass known as Rickert's Pass.

To get to this pass, mountain bikers will be pushing, horses will be slogging, and hikers will be puffing. The climb is 501 m (1,653 ft.) in just 2.5 km (1.5 mi.). In wet weather the trail has a terrible tendency to get mucky, so save this for a sunny day.

The pass was named for an engineer and "con-artist." Julius Rickert discovered coal near the base of the pass in 1902, and managed to interest Pat Burns in potentially developing the site. The mine never succeeded, and it now sits abandoned at the base of the pass. To the early native travellers, this was known as the "many porcupines trail," due to an abundance of this prickly rodent.

From the pass, the trail drops down the south side, and makes a beeline towards Highway 40, arriving there at kilometre 12 (mile 7.2).

Index

Reference

Information

Emergency Contacts
- Kananaskis Country 24-Hour Emergency Response: (403) 591-7767
- R.C.M.P. 24-Hour Emergency Response: (403) 591-7707
- Reporting Forest Fires (Call Collect) (403) 427-3473
- Report a Poacher: 1–800–642–3800

Tourist Information
Kananaskis Country, Box 280, Canmore, Alberta, T0L-0M0: (403) 678-5508. This office can answer most specific inquires, but for trail information contact the following information centres:

Kananaskis Valley Area
- Barrier Lake Visitor Information Centre: (403) 673-3985
- Peter Lougheed Provincial Park: (403) 591-6344
- Smith–Dorrien/Spray Trail Information Centre: (403) 591-6344
- Bow Valley Provincial Park: (403) 673-3663

Elbow/Sheep Area
- Elbow Valley Visitor Information Centre: (403) 949-4261
- Canmore/Kananaskis Chamber of Commerce: (403) 678-4094. They can provide general information on tourism in the Canmore/Kananaskis area.

Accommodation
- Lodge at Kananaskis/Hotel Kananaskis: (403) 591-7711
- Kananaskis Inn: (403) 591-7500
- Mount Engadine Lodge: (403) 678-4080
- Rafter Six Ranch Resort: (403) 673-3622
- Kananaskis Guest Ranch: (403) 673-3737
- Ribbon Creek Hostel: (403) 591-7333

Camping
Highway 40
- Sundance Lodges: (403) 591-7122
- Mount Kidd R.V. Park: (403) 591-7700

Peter Lougheed Provincial Park/Eau Claire Areas:
- Kananaskis Camping Inc.: (403) 591-7226

Bow Valley Provincial Park/Trans Canada Highway Areas:
- Bow Valley Campgrounds Ltd.: (403) 673-2163

Elbow River Valley Area:
- Elbow Valley Campgrounds Inc.: (403) 949-3132

Golfing
- Kananaskis Golf Course Tee Times: (403) 591-7272

Horse Rides/ Pack Trips
- Boundary Ranch (Guinn Outfitters): (403) 591-7171
- Rafter Six Ranch Resort: (403) 673-3622
- M & M Ranch (Bragg Creek): (403) 949-3272
- Anchor D Guiding & Outfitters (Black Diamond): (403) 933-2867

Hunting
- Boundary Ranch (Guinn Outfitters): (403) 591-7171
- Anchor D Guiding & Outfitters: (403) 933-2867

Rafting
- Mirage Adventure Tours: (403) 591-7773
- Rainbow Riders: (403) 850-3686
- Chinook River Sports: 1-800-482-4899

Cross–country Skiing
- Canmore Nordic Centre: (403) 678-2400

Dog Sledding
- Snowy Owl Dogsled Tours: (403) 678-4369
- Howling Dog Sled Dog Tours: (403) 678-9588

Recommended Reading
Cameron, Ward. *Mountain Biking the Canadian Rockies.* Helena, Montana: Falcon Press, 1996.

Chandler, S. et al. *Birds of North America.* New York, New York: Golden Press, 1966.

Daffern, Gillean. *Kananaskis Country Trail Guide:* Calgary, Alberta: Rocky Mountain Books, 1985.

Gadd, Ben. *Handbook of the Canadian Rockies.* Jasper, Alberta: Corax Press, 1988.

Godfrey, Earl W. *The Birds of Canada.* Ottawa, Ontario: Supply and Services Canada, 1976.

Herrero, Stephen. *Bear Attacks—Their Causes and Avoidance.* New York, New York: Winchester Press, 1985.

Kananaskis Country. *The Kananaskis Country Environmental Education Library.* Canmore, Alberta: Kananaskis Country, c. 1988.

Karamitsanis, Aphrodite. *Place Names of Alberta—Volume 1…Mountains, Mountain Parks and Foothills.* Calgary, Alberta: University of Calgary Press, 1991.

Lepp, Gerhardt and Eastcott, Doug. *Backcountry Biking in the Canadian Rockies.* Calgary, Alberta: Rocky Mountain Books, 1993.

Oltmann, C. Ruth. *The Valley of Rumours...the Kananaskis.* Seebe, Alberta: Ribbon Creek Publishing Co., 1976.

Patterson, Bruce. *Alberta. An Altitude SuperGuide.* Banff, Alberta: Altitude Publishing, 1992.

Pole, Graeme. *Canadian Rockies. An Altitude SuperGuide.* Canmore, Alberta: Altitude Publishing, 1992.

Scoter, George W. and Flygare, Hälle. *Wildflowers of the Canadian Rockies.* Edmonton, Alberta: Hurtig Publishers, 1986.

Sheep River Historical Society. *In The Light of the Flares.* Turner Valley, Alberta: Friesen Printers, 1979.

Van Tighem, Kevin. *Wild Animals of Western Canada.* Canmore, Alberta: Altitude Publishing, 1996.

Acknowledgements

Special thanks to Susan Baker, who gave the author the strength and encouragement to keep going. Many thanks to the following people for their invaluable assistance in the completion of this book: Ian Waugh, Eric Kuhn, Ron Chamney, and Scott Maier of Kananaskis Country, The Staff of the Kananaskis Visitor Centre, The Whyte Museum of the Canadian Rockies, The Glenbow Museum Archives, The Canmore Centennial Museum, Mike Mitrovic of Mirage Sports, Jules Leboeuf of the Alberta Forest Service, Laurieanne Lynne of Shell Canada, and many others.

Photographic Credits

All photographs are taken by the author except:

Glenbow Archives, Calgary, Alberta
32 (NA-2736-1); 33 (NA-4139-3); 34 (NA-4002-16); 35 (NA-5124-22); 62 (NA-4824-2); 78 (NA-695-32); 90 (NA-695-1); 92 (NA-695-39); 133 (NA-2468-36); 137 (NA-695-29); 140 (NA-152-1); 146 (NA-4386-1)

Carole Harmon
40

Don Harmon
13

Kananaskis Country Photo Collection
46; 48; 53; 55; 130 (top)

Mirage Adventures
51

Dennis Schmidt
front cover (inset), 17; 20 (top right); 22 (top middle); 23 (top right, middle right); 24 (top middle, top right, middle left); 25 (left and right); 26 (left, middle); 60 (bottom); 94 (bottom); 116; 118; 120; 123; 147

Esther Schmidt
22 (top left); 23 (top left, top middle, bottom right); 24 (top left, bottom left); 25 (middle); 26 (right); 27 (middle); 67 (bottom); 82; 108; 131; 134

About the Author

Ward Cameron

WARD CAMERON has spent many years in the Kananaskis. In 1983, he was hired as an Interpretive Naturalist. In 1986, he began helping in the management of the various Information Centres within the boundaries of Kananaskis Country. He left the public service in 1989 to work as a freelance naturalist and historian, and since that time has spent an increasing amount of time showing groups the riches of the Kananaskis.

His photographs routinely appear in Kananaskis Country brochures and posters. He has done extensive work as a photographer and author for Alberta Tourism. In order to sell his photographs, Ward began writing magazine articles. This has now expanded into a growing writing business. For five years, he wrote a weekly natural and human history column in the Canmore Leader Newspaper, and currently writes feature articles for a variety of magazines. He is the author of one other guide book titled: "Mountain Biking the Canadian Rockies." Another focus falls in the area of storytelling. The history of the west is filled with adventure, and Ward uses these stories to excite and motivate visitors to the Rockies. As Ward puts it: "The history may be short, but there's no shortage of history."